Bringing It All Together

Language and Literacy in the Multilingual Classroom

Marcia Brechtel

DOMINIE PRESS
Pearson Learning Group

To Linnea with love. Everything present in this book is a result of our work together on this model. Without her constant encouragement, support, and faith in me, I would not even have attempted to put our model in print.
To Bill, Josh, and Andy with love. Their patience and support were always there, weekend after weekend.

With special thanks to the people without whose support and encouragement, neither the model nor the book would exist: Kaye Rockwood, Fern Williams, Bob Vanderpool, Jerry Bollinger, Judy Diaz, Martha Martini, and Barbara Causee.
Thanks also go to the great principals, teachers, and students of Fountain Valley School District.

Executive Editor: Carlos Byfield
Copy Editor: Becky Colgan
Cover Designer: Lois Stanfield, Lightsource Images
Layout: Communication Strategies

This book was previously published with the title *Bringing the Whole Together.*

ISBN 1-56270-030-8
Printed in Singapore by PH Productions Pte Ltd
3 4 5 6 7 8 9 10   PH   08 07 06 05 04

Dominie Press

Pearson Learning Group

1-800-321-3106
www.pearsonlearning.com

Table of Contents

Foreword

It was written in 1965, in New Zealand, that there were few things certain about compulsory schooling, but two of the most important were that it was one of the greatest adventures undertaken by humanity and that it was only the uncertain beginning of what would be a long evolution.

I first met with Marcia Brechtel in the spring of 1987, when I addressed a "whole language" conference in La Mirada, and again at an all-day in-service in the Fountain Valley School District, where I shared beliefs, principles, and practices used in language-based classrooms in New Zealand. It was an attempt to articulate research in natural language learning and to demonstrate the application of research into classroom practice. Fundamental was the development of environmental contexts that celebrated, respected, and responded to values deeply rooted in children's lives, capable of serving them lifelong.

My feeling was that in the process of "reaching inside of children," trusting them as natural learners, and providing relevant, meaningful contexts for language learning, there was a confirmation of personal beliefs about the treasures in children's minds.

This book links theory and practice in a concise and practical model of an integrated language arts curriculum. It rings with the experience, success, and dedicated classroom practitioners who observed that by teaching this way, new learners of English were enabled to express their understandings of the world around them freely and creatively, and in the process develop proficiency in the English language.

Bringing It All Together is an invitation and a challenge to teachers and administrators to participate in and experience the excitement of this way of teaching and learning.

To the long evolution, the model developed and presented in this book by Marcia, makes a significant contribution.

—Leanna Traill
Language Consultant
Auckland, New Zealand

Preface

"today I just want to write a poem I don't know why we'll I guess because I felt good inside. I'm glade I can share something with somebody."

—Bianca, 3rd grade

Shortly after publication of the first printing of *Bringing It All Together*, the Guided Language Experience Process (GLEP) became the Guided Language Acquisition Design (GLAD). This happened for a number of reasons. In 1991, after a rigorous process, GLEP was declared Exemplary by the California Department of Education and, later that year, a Project of Academic Excellence, by the U.S. Department of Education, OBEMLA (Office of Bilingual Education and Minority Language Affairs). It was unanimously agreed that GLAD was infinitely preferable to GLEP as an acronym. Concomitantly, the U.S. Department of Education required us to train teachers around the nation. To this date, and it changes daily, we have trained teachers at over 100 school sites nationally: Michigan, Kansas, Texas, Oregon, and Arizona, to name a few states. We can say with all confidence that the strategies we share with you have worked with students in urban, suburban, and rural settings, with special needs students of all sorts (ELL, GATE, special education) and the "regular" students throughout the nation.

This model started in the Fountain Valley School District about seventeen years ago. My partner and I brought to the district varied teaching experiences—Peace Corps, reading specialist, special education, Title I, overseas ESL, regular education, and administration. Faced with the series of unconnected, trivial pictures and grammar structures that was the ESL curriculum in those days, as well as the challenge of students coming from thirty-six to forty different language backgrounds we realized that we had to think "outside of the box."

There have been some changes, updates, and refinements since the last publication. However, our commitment to teaching and learning has not wavered, and can best be summed up in the words of Paulo Friere: "There is no possibility of teaching without learning as there is no possibility of learning without teaching." We have continued to stretch the model and ourselves with new research and writings in the field. We have continued to translate that research into the classroom and let the practice in the classroom influence our research. We hope you enjoy this revised edition and that it helps you stretch and grow in your classroom.

1

Introduction

What it is

Bringing It All Together is designed for teachers in multilingual settings, including both beginning ELD and SDAIE (Specially Designed Academic Instruction in English) level English Language Learners. The concept of unit planning for integration and interrelationship and the use of language acquisition strategies is not limited to the ELD classroom. Today, many native speakers of English come to school without the background knowledge or language skills necessary to make sense of the printed word. All of the ELD strategies described in this book promote language and thus are useful in all classrooms.

Overview

Bringing It All Together is user friendly. It is written in five sections:

- A brief summary of the research that has influenced this model and its implications for teachers
- The model itself, which comprises an organizational structure to *bring together* all the elements for an integrated, research/standards-based unit

- Sample units, which are written at three general grade levels
- A chapter on strategies that defines and describes how to use the definitive strategies of the model
- Appendices that include a glossary of terms and sample daily lesson plans

Research and writings in the field

This chapter provides a brief survey of pertinent theories and writings in the field that have influenced the Guided Language Acquisition Design (GLAD) model, the implications for teachers, and some recommended readings. As teachers, we have a responsibility to know *why* things work as well as *what* things work. This is especially true now, with public education being pilloried. We must be able to clearly articulate our pedagogy to parents, administrators, and the community at large. Since space constraints impede an in-depth study of the research, recommended readings are included to reinforce the survey.

The Guided Language Acquisition Design model

This chapter provides the reader with the empty model for unit planning and instructions on how to use it. It is an important chapter, since without it the sample units would not be meaningful. The chapter includes a generic unit plan. It helps teachers in collaborative groups to do planning for the richest units. This section allows us to ensure that all skills are taught and practiced.

Sample units

The next chapter shows what the unit planning looks like when completed. There is a science unit, a social studies unit, and a literature-based unit. Due to limitations of space, only one subunit (Reptiles) has all the standards and framework references written out. Because of the flexible nature of these units, they can be done at different grade levels. You, of course, would tailor the framework and standards to your grade level. Think whole-unit planning here, not daily lessons.

Strategies

This chapter contains a variety of strategies with specific instructions on *how* and *when* to use them.

Appendices

The appendices include a glossary of terms and several examples of weeklong daily sample lesson plans to demonstrate how the model can be used on a day-to-day basis. The appendices should provide some sense of the interrelated nature of the components and their flow during a unit. These plans cover a span of grades. The appendices also include some tried topics and resources.

Words cannot express how exciting it is to teach this way. You will go home excited, as will your students. You will get wonderful comments from parents, who love to see their children excited about learning. Unit planning will actually reduce your planning time. Find someone to work with and share your excitement and planning; it reduces the workload and is more fun. Start the strategies in small increments so that you are not too overwhelmed. With supportive principals, you will have a wonderful classroom.

Good Luck!

2

Research and Writings in the Field

Professional educators need to keep abreast of current information and research. In this day of public education scrutiny, it is crucial that teachers be able to articulate *how* they teach and *why* they teach that way. Research can also assist teachers in *adjusting* what they do, to meet the needs of the students in their class. It prevents teachers from becoming "dinosaurs," people who have taught the same way for twenty years, and claim that it's just "the same old merry-go-round." With an understanding of brain research, to name one area, we realize why many strategies come around again, but with some refinement or adaptations.

Professionals who are overworked and harried, however, cannot always easily decide which areas of research should be explored, let alone find materials of interest and the time to read them. This chapter gives a brief summary of the research that helped to modify and refine GLAD. It also provides a short list of recommended readings that are pertinent to the following areas:

- Second language acquisition
- Primary language and cultural respect
- Brain research
- Reading and writing research and writings in the field
- What a research-based unit should include

Second language acquisition

Several areas of research have influenced this model, beginning with the research done by Stephen Krashen as a point of departure, and continuing through, for example, the Collier/Thomas report. Some key aspects considered are

A. Language is acquired, not learned—Language is acquired by meaningful immersion, demonstration, and opportunities to practice (Krashen, Cambourne).
B. Comprehensible input—Do not assume that what you say, repeat, or write on the board, is understood. Check that you are understood (Krashen, Cummins).
C. A low affective filter—Develop a classroom where high self-esteem, low anxiety, and inclusion for students are the norm (Krashen, Cummins, Baron, Sagor, and Wink).
D. Negotiating for meaning, comprehensible output, guided oral practice, zone of proximal development and scaffolding—Students need opportunities to use new vocabulary and concepts with someone they understand, and this is usually not the teacher (Long, Swain, Cummins, Vygotsky).
E. Academic language—Teach cognitively demanding, complex concepts and language. Teach to the highest common denominator (Shefelbine, Collier/Thomas).
F. Pull-out programs—The least effective method for elementary settings (Berman, Collier/Thomas).
G. Teacher- and student-generated text—What students can say and understand, they can write or dictate; what they can write or dictate, they can learn to read. How to produce truly leveled reading (ELD Standards, Brechtel/Haley, Van Allen).

Implications for teachers

- Utilize the new standards—they will help integrate and focus teaching.
- Pull-out ESL is not effective. It tends to fragment learning and students.
- New information is provided in a meaningful, comprehensible way that creates a risk-taking environment.
- Direct experiences, visuals, gestures, rephrasing and changes of register assist in comprehension.
- Use students' background information, previous experience, and student-set purpose to connect to new learning.
- Allow time for students to "negotiate for meaning"—use, discuss, and own new concepts and vocabulary.
- Understand and use strategies for students in the "silent period."
- Encourage risk taking in language, limit overcorrecting.
- Ensure that language is used interactively—vary the groupings for scaffolding.
- Teach ELD through the content areas. Make the content challenging and the vocabulary and sentence structure academic. This *must* be done in a comprehensible way. Just using "big words" will not suffice.

Primary language

There is ample research to validate the concept that the stronger children are in their first language, the more academically successful they will be in the second. Previously, and in certain subject areas, academicians have referred to this notion as "background information" or "prior knowledge." However, when applied to second language acquisition, what a student brings to the learning environment is often overlooked (Cummins, Ramirez, Collier/Thomas).

Although new laws in some places restrict instruction in primary language, it is imperative to understand its importance in a child's academic development.

Cross-cultural respect and sensitivity

An important part of this issue is teacher-student interaction. Cummins, Berman, Baron, Sagor, and many others forcefully make the point that no matter what language is used for instruction, if the personal culture, experiences, and language are not validated, the result is alienation from the entire educational process. This feeling of alienation is the biggest reason for drop out rates. (Cummins, Berman). Joan Wink (*Critical Pedagogy; Notes from the Real World*) articulately describes the classrooms where the "culture of silencing" occurs, subtly but completely. We let students know that their culture or language is not acceptable. Our students then conform by closing themselves and their minds down. Clearly, in a multilingual classroom, it is not possible to become an expert on all cultures and their variations. However, teachers can draw upon the expertise available in the classroom with students from a rich variety of cultural backgrounds, and provide opportunities for students to share from their personal life experiences.

The other part of the issue is student-student interactions. The classroom should be a place where students examine and value diversity, similarities, and personal cultural experiences of their own and others. Celebrating holidays and eating ethnic food are not enough to build respect in the classroom. Respect is engendered when students learn to work together successfully and get to know each other beyond the stereotypes they bring to the classroom. Strategies that develop habits of positive interaction are crucial.

Implications for teachers—Primary language and cross-cultural

- Include lots of printed materials (literature, charts, and reference materials) in various languages. This is not "bilingual education" and, unfortunately, will not make your students bilingual. It does say that their language is a valued part of the classroom.
- Utilize the 10/2 with primary language. Even with new laws, this is a permissible use. Primary language for clarification, less than 20 percent of the day, is acceptable.
- Include multicultural literature. However, read it before using it. With the push in the new English Language Arts Framework on diverse literature, many so-called "multicultural" pieces are written by people who are not from the culture and have little or no factual information.
- Do not save *multicultural awareness* for multicultural week, once a year. Embed cross-cultural themes into your units, utilize strategies like cooperative learning with the T-graph for social skills, or personal interaction. Build habits of positive interdependence.
- Do observe holidays by sharing personal and cultural experiences of your students. Let them share what their family does, not what an entire country does. (How does your family celebrate the Lunar New Year? As opposed to: How do people in Vietnam celebrate the New Year?)

Recommended readings

Krashen and Terell, *The Natural Approach*. Alemany Press. 1983.
Collier/Thomas, "Longitudinal Study of Successful Programs for Second Language Learners," 1991.
J. Cummins, *Affirming Diversity*.

Joan Wink, *Critical Pedagogy, Notes From the Real World*.
California State Department of Education, English Language
  Development Standards, 1999.

Brain research

*My second-grade daughter has changed from a second grader who is
kind of going to school to learn to read, to one who is focused and
excited about learning. She asks questions and picks out scads of books
from the library on that theme.*

—Quote from a teacher

Metacognition

The exciting thing about current research and writings in the field
of metacognition is that there is so much consensus across
disciplines. Thinking about one's own thinking, as Art Costa (1987,
Workshop FVSD) phrases it, is a crucial skill to be taught and
modeled constantly for students. In today's world, it is impossible
to supply students with all the information they will need. It is
possible, however, to teach and provide them with opportunities to
practice problem-solving and decision-making skills. It is crucial for
students to understand when they approach a new problem that
they should figure out what they already know about it, decide what
is important to know, what they don't know, where they can find
answers, and what they will do with it once they have it. Art Costa's
10/2 is an excellent strategy for ongoing metacognitive discussions
student to student.

   In reading, Dorothy Strickland talks about the tendency of
teachers to play the "main idea guessing game." We test for
comprehension ("What is the main idea here?") rather than model
metacognitively how we arrived at the answer. It is the modeling
and practice that results in teaching, not testing comprehension
(Costa, Farr).

Making information retrievable

Susan Kovalik (1984–86, FVSD training) first influenced our thinking in the area of retrievable information. Since then, many other writings on brain-compatible teaching have reinforced the importance of patterning. Patterning can be visual, as with graphic organizers, or oral/aural, as with chants, poems and songs. The more meaningful, tied to student's purpose or life experiences, and/ or emotional, the greater the retention.

Kovalik, and more recently, the work of several neurological centers such as the University of California at Irvine, have reinforced the importance of the growth of dendrites and axions connecting brain cells. These are developed through interactive, kinesthetic learning and adult to child conversations starting in infancy.

Right/left brain, multiple intelligences, modalities

Research in these areas, although contested by some or phrased differently by others, is fairly consistent in the idea that humans approach learning differently. This is an important aspect to remember when we are planning our units. "Have I included strategies that allow access to core curricula for my divergent learners?" When we are direct teaching or when students are practicing new concepts, strategies such as team tasks, chants, and the pictorial input chart allow all students to participate successfully.

Implications for teachers

- Actively involve the learner, instead of only accepting the correct answer—ask the student how he/she arrived at the answer.
- Model that same behavior when you teach and arrive at answers.
- Provide students with strategies to organize thinking, such as graphic organizers.

- Recognize, value, and encourage discussions of personal and cultural background or experience. Assist students to see the connections between these and the new knowledge they are learning.
- Apply strategies such as the inquiry charts and KWL, which not only activate and focus background information but also develop a set purpose to the teaching.
- Provide books with predictable pattern or rhyme to facilitate reading and learning.
- Use graphic organizers, such as the pictorial input chart, that imprint information in a pattern that makes · learning retrievable over a long period of time.
- Strategies that utilize music, art, and chants, linked to the content, can assist students with learning. Other strategies that take advantage of different modalities and intelligences allow for differentiation of instruction and access to rigorous curricula for the divergent learner.

Recommended Readings

Newsweek; February 18, 1988

Time; November 1997

Gardner, Multiple Intelligences, 1993

Costa, Art, "What Human Beings Do When They Behave Intelligently . . .", Cal. State University, Sacramento

Lazear, David, *Seven Ways of Knowing*, 1991

Reading and writing

These are very hard words for me, but the way I am learning them is fun. It makes it easier. Thank you.

— Jennifer, 6th grade, Special Education

The following is a brief summary of reading research that has influenced this model. It is not complete, considering that when a person has taught for over 30 years, many different approaches and researchers will have influenced his or her pedagogy. This is as it should be. Over the years, however, teaching literacy seems to have presented a major challenge. It is where our second language learners lose ground. Helping students develop literacy became especially crucial as older students entered our program as illiterates in the first and second language. What we found was that strategies and approaches designed and normed on English-speaking children often did not take into account the need for background information and academic vocabulary that our second language learners had. This is true even today. Many state documents and basal series give token recognition to the need for strategies that meet the needs of the English language learner: "Have a discussion," "Use pictures," "Talk about the book," and "Use cooperative learning" are a few taken straight out of these documents. Nothing is said on why, when, or how these strategies should be used. As Shefelbine (Remarks: IRA 1999, California Literature Project, 1998) has often stated, one program will never meet everyone's needs. It takes the teacher to make the diagnosis and teach to it. Many of us have been out there struggling to help our students achieve academic literacy with little or no help.

In a later chapter, this book will share with you some of the strategies we have used in reading and writing that have resulted in over twelve years of standardized test scores in reading and language that have exceeded the norm. One of the most important keys here is balance in the classroom. There should be a balance of total class modeling, small group practice, and then individual use. This allows for much needed scaffolding for our English language learner.

Implications for teachers

- Provide reading that stresses the purpose and joy of reading for students who are struggling. Begin with writing and reading their own language (student generated texts).
- Provide immense amounts of reading to students; time for silent sustained reading and silent sustained writing, with oral book sharing and quick shares.
- Access students' background information and show them how it connects to the new learnings (ELD Standards,1999; California Reading Task Force, 1995/96; Krashen (Second Language Acquisition), Flores, 1973; Goodman, *The Psycholinguistic Nature of the Reading Process,* 1973; Traill, Remarks: FVSD 1987–89).
- Direct teaching of concepts, academic vocabulary, complex sentence structure, and skills. Doing so comprehensibly is the point we often miss as teachers.
- Offer a lot of modeling and a chance to practice new skills and concepts, in groups first, in order to provide opportunities for scaffolding for success.
- Make available opportunities for students to negotiate for meaning with other students (Vygotsky, UCI Writing Project, Betances, Long, Swain, Chall, Reading Task Force, ELA Standards, ELD Standards, Shefelbine, and Adams).
- Teach writing that stresses the metacognitive use of reading and writing as a process. Use clustering/brainstorming/sketching to initiate writing; accept the developmental level of the writer; use mini-lessons and conferencing to practice skills, editing, and revising done in the appropriate places; and publish the piece (Graves, Calkins, UCI Writing Project, Rico, ELA and ELD Standards).

- Use logs to obtain personal responses to texts and issues; interactive journals for dialogue with students; interactive reading and writing, and teacher and student-generated texts for reading; Big Books (teacher and student-made), shared and guided reading and writing; and a language functional wall (Traill, Cummins, Pinell, Goodman, and Butler).
- Practice a balance in the classroom of total class modeling, small group practice and individual use. This balance should be based on student needs, not required numbers. It should be a balance of required reading and writing and student set choice.

Recommended Readings

A. Schifini, "Reading Instruction for the Pre-literate and Struggling Older Student," 1996.

M. Adams, *Beginning To Read*, 1991.

Butler and/or Traill, *Shared and Guided Reading*.

Flood, Lapp, Flood and Nagel; "Using Flexible Patterns for Effective Instruction."

L Calkins, *The Art of Teaching Writing*, 1986.

H. Yopp, "Developing Awareness in Young Children?" *The Reading Teacher*, Vol. 45, 1992.

Classroom environment

Grouping students

Frequently, initial grouping is done very early in a child's school career—usually in kindergarten and first grade. Such groupings, which more likely reflect the family's socioeconomic status or the child's command of English than the child's ability or potential to learn, result in the higher-placed child receiving favored treatment (more frequent and positive interactions with teachers).

Students in low tracks saw their teachers as more punitive and less concerned about them than did other students. They agreed that they felt left out of class activities. They also reported the lowest levels of peer esteem and highest levels of discord in their classes (Goodlad).

Low-track classes devote a much larger share of instructional time to rote learning and the application of knowledge and skills (Goodlad). The Berman/Wyler report and the Collier and Thomas report are clear that second language programs must be taught with cognitively challenging material. Expectations must be kept high.

Understanding the importance of leveled reading groups, it is equally important that students do not also spend the rest of the morning in the "buzzard" group. It is crucial that the groups be flexible and the practice (centers or team tasks) be arranged heterogeneously. This is not difficult at all. If you are using centers or team tasks, make sure the rotations are in heterogeneous groups and remove yourself from the rotation. Thus, instead of calling up the entire red group, call the students you wish by name.

A language-functional environment

Leanna Traill of New Zealand influenced us heavily on the importance of a language functional environment. Walls should be dripping with the language of the students and the content they are learning. Print rich is not sufficient if the students are not using the print. Recent studies of word walls have shown that in classrooms where teachers do not have students interact with the word walls on a daily basis, the wall becomes only so much decoration. We must design strategies that encourage our students to use this resource.

Functional walls are important for another reason. With many of our students coming to school without a literacy background in the home, it means we need to supply those 2,000 hours (rough estimate by Dorothy Strickland, *The Reading Teacher,* ongoing articles) of literacy practice that other students come to school with. Our walls are no longer "cutsie" art bulletin boards or bulletin boards that only display the ten perfect papers. Our walls must drip with the language of academics, built by students and teachers, and used daily by students to help with reading and writing.

Integrated learning

Integration is the model we use to "bring it all together." Listening, speaking, reading, and writing are interrelated and integrated into the curricula. The focus, keeping in mind our second language learners, is meaningful content to promote language and thinking. The focus is also to create connections or links between previously learned information and the new information, links between the content areas, and links among listening, speaking, reading, and writing. We use the idea page to pull all this together. It makes our lives simpler in several ways: (1) If all the students are studying to a larger theme, it is easier to find books at their reading level, (2) The students can then work in heterogeneous groups on similar information about the theme, (3) It allows for peer tutoring and supports cooperative learning, (4) It allows students to study with greater depth and complexity if we spend more time on a theme (as opposed to a book a week), (5) Students learn faster (Kovalik, brain-compatible teaching workshops, GATE workshops and guidelines).

Recommended Readings

Berman et al., "Meeting the Challenge of Language Diversity,"
    California Legislature, 1991.
Goodlad, *A Place Called School.*

Implications for teachers—classroom environment

- Structure flexible groupings to include leveled and heterogeneous reading groups, ELD, SDAIE, GATE, and Expert groups.
- Implement cooperative learning strategies to promote positive interdependence and self-esteem. Students practice in heterogeneous groups to provide scaffolding for concepts and vocabulary.
- Classroom walls are no longer filled with merely cute little art. Rather, the art is combined with the print process, inquiry charts, input charts, and others on a daily basis.
- Read and write on the walls often—we call this focused reading.
- Be aware of the attitude and ambiance you have created in the classroom. Reinforce the positive by using scientist reinforcements and the T-graph for social skills.
- Build a classroom of respect for all. Ask yourself, Do my classroom, behaviors, and rules "silence" the unacceptable child?
- Develop a classroom where environment, academics, and interactions promote feelings of confidence, optimism, belonging, usefulness, and power/potency (Sagor).
- Use the standards, frameworks, and district curricula to let you know what you "must" teach. This is first and foremost. Go to grade level texts for content-based vocabulary.
- Help students see the whole, while studying the parts.

What a research-based unit should include

Research should influence practice, and vice versa. The following ideas, not meant to replace the five-step lesson plan, are things we consider when planning our units.

1. A time to activate, focus, and build background information
    *   Inquiry charts, observation charts, KWL, discussions, brainstorms, clustering

2. Opportunities to ensure a common base of understanding, academic vocabulary
    *   Direct experiences, visuals, teacher read-aloud and teacher-generated text 10/2, negotiating for meaning

3. Student's set purpose for learning
    *   Motivating, stated result or goal; student choices; inquiry charts

4. Chances for negotiating for meaning from language or text
    *   Cooperative activities for scaffolding, heterogeneous groupings, 10/2

5. *Comprehensible*, direct teaching of concepts, vocabulary, complex sentence structure, text patterns, skills
    *   Teacher-made Big Books, graphic organizers, realia, read-aloud, conferences

6. A theme that is embedded into your academic unit that promotes cross-cultural respect, self-esteem, empowerment

7. Classrooms that promote risk-taking, self-awareness, and respect

8. Reading and writing that keeps the second-language learner in mind
    *   Stresses the joy and purpose for reading to struggling readers
    *   Begins with reading and writing student's own language
    *   Immense amounts of reading to students
    *   A language functional classroom
    *   Flexible groupings

- Reading to, with, and by students: a balance of total class modeling, small group practice and then individual use
- Reading and writing strategies that teach skills and strategies that allow those skills to be practiced in a meaningful way

9. Active participation in all components. Use of strategies that involve different modalities and intelligences
   - Chants, poetry, art, music, interviews, surveys, building projects

10. Students deliberately taught and allowed to practice ways to organize thoughts and texts
    - Graphic organizers, text and test formats, and vocabulary

11. Teacher and students modeling and articulating how answers were found, not just what the correct answer was.

12. Ongoing and final assessments and evaluations that teach test-taking skills of standardized formats, allow for personal exploration, alternative means of assessment
    - Student-made Big Books, sketch and listen, use of test language on a daily basis

3

The Guided Language Acquisition Design

My son was really turned on to the joy of learning after his teacher began using this model. I know it works.

— San Jose parent/teacher

This chapter brings it all together in an integrated curriculum. It describes the curriculum model that, for us, was a way to "bring together everything that we had been learning." As should be expected, all our units begin with planning. It is crucial, when differentiating instruction, that teachers have a firm idea of the goals: content, concepts, skills, and assessment. The key to this component of the model is collaboration. Excitement, motivation, and top-notch work are generated when teachers get together to discuss and generate ideas professionally and cooperatively.

Idea pages

The "What Am I Going to Teach?" pages

We plan our units as we work with students, from whole to part. The first section is the *idea pages*. This is where we brainstorm the *what* that we are going to teach. We have written our idea page in outline form; however, it is very easy to develop in graphic organizer format. On the idea pages we brainstorm each and every idea. No editing is done here. Ideas that may not fit this year may fit next year with another set of students.

We have divided the *idea pages* into several components:

- **Theme/themes**: Think—Integration and interrelation of your subjects; cross-cultural themes; self-esteem, enduring understandings
- **Focusing/motivating activities**: Think—Metacognition, access, focus, and value personal experiences build background information
- **Concepts**: Think—frameworks and standards; across curricula; English language learner
- **Vocabulary**: Think—High, academic—teach to the highest, review to the lowest; comprehensible; complex sentence structure, English language learner
- **Skills**: Think—English language arts and math/science/social studies standards, district guidelines; integration, in context; knowing your goal
- **Closure**: Think—Metacognition, personal exploration, rubrics, variety of assessments to meet purpose, ongoing, test-taking formats, and language
- **Resources and materials**: Think—Books, people, community, technology, anything that makes your subject come alive

Unit/cross-cultural theme

The unit theme is identified from grade level core curriculum. The unit theme emphasizes a particular content area such as science, social studies, or literature, while embedding universal or cross-cultural themes. The cross-cultural theme has a focus of promoting interpersonal relations. Celebrating *Cinco de Mayo* is not sufficient for preventing prejudice. One develops respect for another by working together and understanding another's viewpoint. This must be modeled on a daily basis, not only on Chinese New Year.

In a unit centered around *The Island of the Blue Dolphin*: the universal theme of that literature piece might be survival; the science aspect—the survival of the flora and fauna of the Pacific Coast; the cross-cultural theme might be the survival, or genocide, of the Native Californians; and the personal validation might be how we all survive on a daily basis.

Unit theme summary

- Integration of curricula, enduring understandings
- High expectations
- Personal, cultural validation

Focusing and motivation

This component serves several purposes. The most obvious, perhaps, is the metacognitive aspect of accessing background information, focusing on what is important, developing a student's set purpose, building background information, and providing a scaffolding for the students from the known to the new. One key aspect here is the validation of personal and cultural life experiences. This continues the cross-cultural aspect begun with the theme planning. Your Spanish-speaking student is not an expert on every Spanish-speaking culture, nor is your Vietnamese student an expert on all Vietnamese, no more than is your blond, blue-eyed student an expert of the "Leave it to Beaver" American culture that passed away years ago, if it ever existed at all. What your students can be experts on, however, is their own personal life experiences, which includes the individual cultures of each family.

We want, also, to motivate, excite, or interest students in new areas of exploration for them. This component is for us to use an appropriate diagnostic tool to assess the level of background information. We avoid the "spray and pray" method of giving all students everything, regardless of strengths and needs.

Focusing and motivation summary

- Activate, focus, and build background information.
- Validate personal and cultural connection between personal experience and new learning.
- Student sets purpose for learning.
- Diagnosis for teacher
- High interest and relevancy to student

Concepts

In this component, we brainstorm all the concepts, the *big ideas*, the objectives that we want the students to walk away with at the end of the unit. It is important to refer to your frameworks and standards from any and all curricula areas you are integrating. These provide your goal. These are, also, directly tied (or should be) to your assessment and evaluation as well as to your development of all direct teaching strategies, including big books, poetry, and input charts. Teachers need to have a firm idea of what these are.

Concepts summary

- High expectations (no watered-down content)
- Scaffolding—taking students from the known to the new
- Integration of other curricula areas
- Use of standards and frameworks
- Comprehensible direct teaching of concepts

Vocabulary

By listing the vocabulary needs, we keep in mind the linguistic needs of all students within the context of this unit. We will be aware of areas of potential difficulty for our ELL students as well as many others. This listing of key and potentially problematic vocabulary will change from year to year, depending on your students' background information.

Vocabulary summary

- Teach to the highest, review to the beginners, academic language and expectations.
- Remember, complex sentence structure is key to vocabulary.
- Go to your textbooks to find the needed academic language.
- Contextual clues, comprehensible information
- Acquisition of vocabulary as a process
- Use of poetry, input charts, and big books as a means of assisting the development of vocabulary

Skills

Recently, there has been a lot of media attention on whole language versus phonics or skill teaching. The assumption is if you are teaching whole language, you are not using skills. In our case, this is patently absurd. We have always had a place in our planning to list skills that are generated from state, district, and grade-level standards.

The new ELD standards help the teacher to recognize and teach to the needs of the ELL because skills are also derived from the linguistic needs of your students. As such, these skills will vary from year to year. One year, your students may not need initial consonants or main idea, the next year, the students will be different and so will their needs. Your skill teaching is directly connected to your assessment of the students.

Shefelbine reiterates that direct teaching of *phonics* is essential, and the easiest to teach. Teaching, and not assessing, academic language and higher level thinking skills is much more difficult and often ignored. Academic language and complex sentence structure must be taught and practiced in a meaningful way.

We brainstorm skills in the area of English language arts as well as any other content area that has been integrated. This is why, in an integrated unit, certain skills lend themselves to being easily taught in context. For example, superlative and comparative adjectives are effectively taught in a tall tales unit or comparative fairy tales.

Skills summary

- Direct and comprehensible teaching of skills
- Skills developed from standards and needs of students
- Skills practiced in context
- Decoding skills kept simple, taught in context—good literature
- Higher level thinking skills
- Academic language and sentence structure
- Go to ELA and ELD standards

Closure

This component entails the end of the unit evaluation strategies that will be utilized for this unit. "What will the students do to show me what they have acquired?" "How will we develop the rubric, so that there is no 'hidden test'?" Keep in mind that the ultimate evaluation is not just "what do I know?" but "what will I do with it?"

We have found that team explorations of a subject provide a low-anxiety way to initiate the assessment or evaluation process. It provides some team modeling and practice of developing a project to a rubric.

We feel a personal commitment to types of assessment where the student chooses a method that will show us what he/she has acquired. Just as there are multiple intelligences, so students need to be provided with options on ways to show what they have acquired. Some students might choose songs or poetry; some might choose to build a project, others to write an expository essay. This is where student/teacher-developed rubrics provide a clear understanding on both parts of expectations and evaluation.

Portfolios and other means of authentic assessment give us a well-rounded view of growth over time. We have found them invaluable when conferencing with students and parents. We do, however, give students experiences with the format of a standardized, or multiple-choice exam. We feel strongly that students can be taught to take tests without fear or too much anxiety (reinforced by Wiggins and Sagor, Remarks: CASCD, 1999). Test-taking skills are important. Our students will be taking tests for the rest of their lives. If we can teach them to approach them without fear, we will indeed be passing on a useful skill. As teachers, however, we need to realize the limitations of such tests for diagnosis. They will give us a very limited picture of what the student has acquired. Our responsibility is to decide which assessment/evaluation tool will meet the purpose for giving it (and all assessment should have some purpose): diagnosis, ongoing assessment, summative evaluation, measurement against a norm, or criteria. Today with standards-based instruction we should ask ourselves why this is being measured on a norm-referenced test, which by definition changes, as students become more successful. We as teachers need to know the pros and cons of various assessment tools and be able to explain them to parents (and, sometimes, administrators).

Closure and evaluation summary

- Personal exploration (student choice with rubrics)
- Team exploration (low risk)
- Authentic and/or alternative means of assessment
- Teacher/student developed rubrics
- Teaching of test-taking skills, format, and testing language

Resources and materials

We have found this to be an invaluable section. Include community resources, parents, guest speakers, videos, laser discs, and books. The more you add here, the more valuable these materials become. Brainstorming resources with other teachers pools the expertise and knowledge of books.

Resources and materials summary

- Primary language resources
- Variety of print and media
- Community resources
- What my parents can do, rather than what they cannot do

Unit planning pages

The "How Am I Going to Teach It" pages

The second section of the two-part planning is called the *planning pages*. It is here that teachers brainstorm various strategies that will allow them to deliver comprehensible information that students acquire easily. This is still a brainstorming section. You may not use every strategy every year, but this allows you variety as well as the capability to differentiate your instruction to meet the needs of your students each year. The key here is to remember that the GLAD model is not a flat one. We do not do a prescribed number of minutes everyday of every strategy. The strategies are designed with a flow, based on the needs of the students. Keeping your second language learners in mind, at the beginning of a unit, the teacher is the one who knows the concepts and vocabulary to be taught. Therefore, the kinds of strategies are more teacher-based. The teacher knows best how to make these comprehensible. However, as the unit progresses, the emphasis switches from content-based teacher talk to students—talking, reading, and writing in the content area.

Two of the components carry over from the idea pages. The components of the planning pages consist of the following:

1. Focusing and motivation
2. Input
3. Guided oral practice
4. Reading/writing activities
5. Extended activities for integration
6. Closure/evaluation

Focusing and motivation

Just as with the *idea pages*, brainstorm all the meaningful, student-centered experiences that access background information. Personal involvement and personal and cultural validation are key here. Academically, these provide the bridge between what is known to what is new.

Whereas the idea pages will have the one "big bang" idea to start your whole unit, these pages will also have ideas and strategies to keep your students focused and motivated during a unit.

Use of positive reinforcement is a part of GLAD. These are not used to reward levels of cognitive answers (yours is better than hers), but rather to teach and reinforce standards for behavior. All reinforcements are directly tied to vocabulary or concepts being taught. All these strategies lead to the students' ability to recognize, articulate, and produce positive social skills such as making good decisions, problem solving, and showing respect. Super scientists' reinforcements are one example. Using the T-graph for social skills is another example of behavior management strategies for group work with emphasis on the positive.

Focusing and motivation summary

- Daily, ongoing
- Activate, focus, and build background information, prior knowledge, schema
- Connect personal and cultural experiences to new knowledge
- Set student purpose for learning
- Diagnose students' current information and skill level
- Spark interest and excitement

Sample strategies and activities for focusing and motivation

- Use inquiry charts, observation charts, and KWL charts.
- Use teacher-made Big Books.
- Practice personal interaction.
- Use direct, interactive experiences such as science explorations, field trips, guest speakers, real things, laser discs, videos, drama, picture files, cooking.
- Use ongoing predicting charts, processing all charts.

Input

This component is for brainstorming strategies that one can use when there are concepts, skills, information, or text patterns that need to be taught directly. There is a place for direct teaching in almost any unit that is being taught at a bit beyond what the students already know. These strategies take advantage of visuals, graphic organizers, realia, active participation, and patterning to make information retrievable over a long period of time. Using pictorial input charts is highly effective. Information and concepts are presented as the teacher draws a visual representation (predrawn in pencil so that the teacher can keep up the pace and take advantage of brain imprinting). All lectures should be broken up by time for informal processing by students. Art Costa refers to this as a 10/2 lecture. A teacher should never talk longer than ten minutes without giving the students two minutes to process with a partner. To deliver these strategies effectively, the teacher must be aware of content and linguistic needs of the students within this particular content. The key here is to build academic language, sentence structures, and concepts.

Input summary

- Practice direct teaching of skills, concepts, text patterns, and academic language and structure.
- Use patterning, visuals, graphics, multimedia, real items, field trips, experts in the field, hands-on, active participation, anything.
- Use 10/2 lecture to provide negotiating for meaning and comprehensible output.

Sample input strategies

- Teacher-made Big Books
- Narrative and pictorial input charts
- Graphic organizers of all kinds
- Read aloud from all kinds of texts, expository as well as narrative
- Use of realia, science explorations, videos, films, and technology
- The 10/2 lecture

Guided oral practice

Based on the works of Swain, Cummins, Vygotsky, Long, and Kagen, this component is a crucial part, if information is to be truly internalized by the student and not just memorized. However, in search for a "quiet" classroom, we often silence our students, most often the students who most need the scaffolding. Students must have time for negotiating for meaning, comprehensible output, or discussions, using new vocabulary and concepts with someone they understand.

Teachers need to set up these activities to promote habits of positive interdependence and to allow students to process, problem solve and develop cross-cultural respect by working together. This is not a time for testing. This is the time for scaffolding for success. We too often jump to assessment, when our students need practice with someone they understand (Surprise! It may not be us!). This is called scaffolding.

Guided oral practice summary

- Give students a chance to negotiate for meaning with others at all levels.
- Allow for scaffolding, processing, internalizing of vocabulary and concepts.
- Provide low affective filter and help extend vocabulary.
- Develop social and problem-solving skills through successful use of content-based recognition of personal growth, cooperative learning and the T-graph for social skills.
- Encourage students to bring their own experiences to the meaning of literature and new concepts.

Sample strategies and activities for guided oral practice

- A perfect component for cooperative learning activities: numbered heads together, picture file activities, expert groups, team projects, reports, discussions, and debates
- Personal interaction
- Poetry, chanting, songs, reader's theater, role playing
- The sentence patterning chart known as the Farmer in the Dell
- Process grid

31

Reading and writing

We feel strongly about the classroom being a place of balance: a balance between cooperative and individual work and a balance between total class modeling, cooperative or small group practice, and individual practice. These activities, although listed separately from guided oral practice, are actually used interchangeably. Listening, discussing, reading, and writing should be taught and used in a natural flow as students study new concepts.

The total class modeling comes from the work of the UCI writing project, which demonstrates that teacher modeling of authentic writing does not occur enough, considering how powerful it is. It replaces the creative writing of the "old days," where we wrote the ten things on the board that students needed to have in their writing and where writing itself was never modeled for the students. Strategies like the group frame and cooperative strip paragraph allow teachers to teach language arts and writing skills as well as to model the editing process. When brainstorming, do we as teachers model what we do when we can't spell a word? When we are taking dictation or writing for the group, do we verbalize the mechanics we are using, such as question marks, exclamation marks, indenting? Many of the mechanics of writing are easily acquired if they are modeled while verbalizing instead of being taught out of context.

It is equally important to present a large number of team/small group activities. We have seen the advantages of flexible groupings. Groups are formed according to the activity and based on the needs of the activity and the students. A few of the strategies should include lots and lots of reading and writing of their own language, partner reading, ear-to-ear reading, focused reading (reading the walls), choral reading, cooperative strip paragraphs, team worksheets, team mind-maps, read-arounds, three-before-me-editing, oral book sharing, and poetry booklets.

The last section is Individual Reading and Writing, which provides opportunities for free choice reading and writing. Drop everything and read time (DEAR time) or silent sustained reading, learning logs, interactive journals, reading/writing workshop, text readings with SQ3R and DRTA, and computers are some options here. The key to remember in this section is that if it has been modeled by the teacher authentically, practiced in groups, then the teacher has raised the success level for the students.

Reading and writing summary

- Allow for a balance of teacher total class modeling, small group (cooperative) practice for scaffolding, and individual use.
- Model and teach a variety of text patterns (expository as well as narrative).
- Use a variety of text, materials, media, and great literature.
- Use a language functional environment to promote language acquisition, brain-compatible teaching and reading.
- Use flexible groupings and differentiated instruction.

Sample strategies and activities for reading and writing

- Total class modeling
  - Group frame, cooperative strip paragraph, poetry frames, read aloud, shared reading and writing, interactive writing
- Small group scaffolding
  - Cooperative activities: team tasks, team cooperative strip paragraph, team poetry, chants, read-arounds, leveled groups, expert groups, heterogeneous groups, ELD groups, anything teacher modeled
- Individual use
  - Required writing styles, writer's workshop, learning logs, interactive journals, and anything modeled by the teacher and practiced in groups

Extended activities for integration

"Have I reached all the students' modalities or learning styles?" This component, based on brain research, is intended to ensure that we include in our units opportunities for students to participate successfully in a variety of ways: right brain, modalities, learning styles, and multiple intelligences.

Extended activities summary

- Think right brain or nonlinear, visual, art, music.
- Think hands-on, building, manipulating, kinesthetic.
- Use these throughout the unit.
- Include them for your divergent thinker, *different* learner.

Sample of activities for extended component

- Cooking and tasting
- Building models, dioramas, hyperstudio sets
- Plays, puppets, drama, reader's theater
- Songs, chants, poetry, movement
- Solving real-life problems
- Student-made books (with art)
- Collecting folders

Closure and evaluation

"Did they get it?" is a question that we feel should be changed to "Are they getting it?" If you wait until the end of a unit to find out, it is way too late. Teachers deal daily with issues of ongoing assessment. This is the section to not only brainstorm big, end-of-the-unit evaluation, but also to determine what strategies will be used to assess the students on an ongoing basis, including preassessment. A few of the strategies we have used encompass from inquiry charts to portfolios from the writer's workshop, learning logs, team tasks, and self-evaluation. Our favorite team exploration is the student-made big books, where listening, discussion, reading, and writing are integrated with content and fine arts.

We are influenced by the work of Wiggins and Sagor, who state that we too often give the *hidden test*. The required content and nature of the tests should be made known to students and practiced. Teacher and student should develop rubrics based on concepts and vocabulary to be acquired. These will have been brainstormed in *the idea pages*.

A variety of assessment is crucial. Your assessment tool will differ depending on your purpose. There are many excellent books and articles on assessment and evaluation such as *Highlight My Strengths*, by Leanna Traill and the CALLA work done by Chamot and O'Malley (1994). Since assessment is not the focus of this book, we will not discuss it in depth on these pages.

Closure and evaluation summary

- Keep metacognition in mind (how did we arrive at the answer).
- Allow time for personal exploration of the subject.
- Use teacher- and student-made rubrics.
- Allow for alternative means of assessment.
- Process all charts and learning during and at the end of the unit.
- Teach test-taking skills and practice test formats and test language in class.
- End on a positive note.

Sample activities for closure and evaluation

- Individual
  - Personal exploration with rubric
  - Models and projects (teacher-supplied materials)
  - Computer and other multimedia projects
  - "Real tests"
  - Portfolios
  - Sketch and write
  - Learning logs
  - Assessment conferences
- Team
  - Big books
  - Models
  - Plays
  - Videos
  - Computer presentations
  - Pictorial input charts
  - Oral presentations
  - Team-written test questions
  - Team evaluation

4

Sample Units

The sample units in this chapter include the following:

- **Comparative folklore**, a literature-based unit that examines similar folklore from around the world. This subject is generally taught in the third through fifth grades, depending on the folklore chosen.
- **Trip around the world**, a social studies-based unit that examines common threads in human needs and culture. Grade-level suitability depends on sophistication of the concepts of needs and culture. This unit has been used, with adaptations, in second through fifth grades.
- **Life in a Pond**, a science-based unit that centers around the physical, life, and earth science concepts of a pond. This unit has been used in kindergarten through second grade.

Note: As these grade levels are only approximate, you will go to your frameworks, standards, and textbooks for your grade. We have given only a few examples of this.

Comparative folklore

Folklore awakens the feeling of participation with human beings of all nations. Children start to sense that the world is a challenging and wondrous adventure. Heroes and heroines deal with ethical or moral dilemmas that truly cross all cultures. Folklore is a wonderfully appropriate unit to open the year because it encompasses the accumulated art and wisdom of everyday people—nursery rhymes, superstitions, games and songs, ballads, dance, medicinal arts, old tales, verses, proverbs, fables, myths, legends, fairy tales, hero tales, and epics across numerous countries or cultures. Because this knowledge is the product of a preliterate society, comparative folklore is an excellent recognition and reinforcement of the oral tradition.

At a beginning ELD level, comparative folklore may be used as a perfect entry unit. All the basic core vocabulary—body parts, colors, numbers, family—can be taught through the high interest context of folktales. What could be more fun than discussing body parts of trolls and ogres!

At a transitional level, the school year may often be opened using the folklore genre. There are folktales at all reading and interest levels that get the students interested and motivated to read. For transitional teachers who use the basal, it is suggested that they start with folklore to get students reading again after the summer. This will ensure that students will have a heterogeneous, motivating beginning.

Possible variations

- Rags to riches
  - *Cinderella*—France
  - *Ashenputtel*—Germany
  - *Yeh-Shen*—China
  - *The Indian Cinderella*—Canada
  - *Fool of the World and the Flying Ship*—Russia
  - *In the Land of Small Dragon*—Vietnam
  - *Tattercoats*—England
- Small people
  - *Tom Thumb*—England
  - *Thumbelina*—Denmark

- *Issunboshi; Momotaru*—Japan
- *Little One Inch*—Vietnam
- *Pulgarcito*—Mexico
- Explaining the stars
  - *How Grandmother Spider Stole the Sun*—Native American
  - *Star Boy*—Blackfeet Indian
  - *Arrow to the Sun*—Pueblo Indian
  - *Why the Sun and Moon Live in the Sky*—Africa
  - *East of the Moon and West of the Sun*—Norway
  - *The Oldest Stories in the World*—Middle East
  - *How the Sun and the Moon Went Out to Dinner*—India
  - *D'Aulaire Book of Greek Myths*—Greek
  - *Keepers of the Earth*—Native American

GLAD Idea Page
Teaching and Explaining
A Study of Folklore from Different Countries

Unit theme (include folktales, fairy tales, and myths)
Teaching and explaining through the centuries
Subthemes/concepts

Many cultures have similar legends and folktales. Folktales and characters have universal elements and common threads.

Focusing and motivation

- Art activity: Thumbprint characters
- Movie or video of a country or a specific tale
- Artifacts, media, art prints
- Visitors and presentation on their cultures
- Inquiry charts
- Maps
- Teacher-made Big Books on a fairy tale
- Read aloud: One to two pages

- World map bulletin board
- Castle bulletin board: Characters from tales peering out of windows
- Choral reading and reader's theater

Closure activities

- Read *Teeny-Tiny Day* for the small-people unit.
- Share personal explorations.
- Share team Big Books.
- Process charts and learning.
- Perform plays, videos, puppet shows, and others.
- Sketch and write about common elements.
- Write a fairy tale.

Concepts (go to frameworks and standards)

- Fairy tales have magical characters such as fairies, witches, ogres, enchanted people, and royalty (ELA Framework, third/fourth).
- Fairy tales have an introduction (brief, dream world, no time period), a development (universal plots, often three tasks, riddles, or trials, logical), and a conclusion (swift climax, triumphs, evil is punished, often a moral) (ELA Framework, third/fourth).
- All cultures have an oral tradition that results in folklore folktales, fairy tales, myths, legends, nursery rhymes, etc.

Comparison of similarities and difference (ELA Framework, second through sixth)

Vocabulary (go to textbooks)

- Specific vocabulary from specific story and country, such as temple, gods, lords, beautiful, virtuous, princess

- Beginning ELD vocabulary
  - Body parts, clothes, family, houses, feelings

Oral language, reading, and writing skills (Skills would be appropriate to the grade level.)

This sample is based on third/fourth grade skills, based on ELA Standards.

Reading

(+) 1.0 **Word analysis, fluency, and systematic vocabulary development**

Word recognition

(+) 1.1 Read narrative and expository text aloud with grade-appropriate fluency and accuracy and with appropriate spacing, intonation, and expression.

Vocabulary and concept development

(+) 1.2 Apply knowledge of word origins, derivations, synonyms, antonyms, and idioms to determine the meaning of words and phrases.

(+) 1.3 Use knowledge of root words to determine the meaning of unknown words within a passage.

(+) 1.4 Know common roots and affixes derived from Greek and Latin and use this knowledge to analyze the meaning of complex words *(e.g., international).*

(+) 2.0 **Reading comprehension**

Students read and understand grade-level-appropriate material. They draw upon a variety of comprehension strategies as needed.

Structural features of informational materials

(+) 2.1 Identify structural patterns found in informational text.

Comprehension and analysis of grade-level-appropriate text

(+)   2.2   Use appropriate strategies when reading for different purposes (e.g., full comprehension, location of information, personal enjoyment).

(+)   2.3   Make and confirm predictions about text by using prior knowledge and ideas presented in the text itself, including illustrations, titles, topic sentences, important words, and foreshadowing clues.

(+)   2.4   Evaluate new information and hypotheses by testing them against known information and ideas.

(+)   2.5   Compare and contrast information on the same topic after reading several passages or articles.

(+)   2.6   Distinguish between cause and effect and between fact and opinion in expository text.

(+)   2.7   Follow multiple-step instructions in a basic technical manual (e.g., how to use computer commands or video games).

(+)   **3.0   Literary responses and analysis:**

Structural features of literature

(+)   3.1   Describe the structural differences of various imaginative forms of literature, including fantasies, fables, myths, legends, and fairy tales.

Narrative Analysis of Grade-Level-Appropriate Text

(+)   3.2   Identify the main events of the plot, their causes, and the influence of each event on future actions.

(+)   3.3   Use knowledge of the situation and setting and of a character's traits and motivations to determine the causes for the character's action.

(+)   3.4   Compare and contrast tales from different cultures by tracing the exploits of one character type and develop theories to account for similar tales in diverse cultures (e.g., trickster tales).

(+)   3.5   Define figurative language (e.g., simile, metaphor, hyperbole, personification) and identify its use in literary works.

Writing

(+) **1.0   Writing strategies**

Organization and focus
(+)   1.1 Create multiple-paragraph compositions.

Organization and focus
(+)   1.2 Use traditional structures for conveying information (e.g., chronological order, cause and effect, similarity and difference, and posing and answering questions).

Research and technology
(+)   1.3 Quote or paraphrase information sources, citing them appropriately.
(+)   1.4 Locate information in reference texts by using organizational features (e.g., prefaces, appendices).
(+)   1.5 Use various reference materials (e.g., dictionary, thesaurus, card catalog, encyclopedia, on-line information) as an aid to writing.
(+)   1.6 Understand the organization of almanacs, newspapers, and periodicals and how to use those print materials.

Evaluation and revision
(+)   1.7 Edit and revise selected drafts to improve coherence and progression by adding, deleting, consolidating, and rearranging text.

(+) **2.0   Writing applications (genres and their characteristics)**
(+)   2.1 Write narratives.
(+)   2.2 Write information reports.
(+)   2.3 Write summaries that contain the main ideas of the reading selection and the most significant details.

Written and oral English language conventions

(+) **1.0 Written and oral English language conventions**
Sentence structure
- (+) 1.1 Use simple and compound sentences in writing and speaking.
- (+) 1.2 Combine short, related sentences with appositives, participial phrases, adjectives, adverbs, and prepositional phrases.

Grammar
- (+) 1.3 Identify and use regular and irregular verbs, adverbs, prepositions, and coordinating conjunctions in writing and speaking.

Punctuation
- (+) 1.4 Use parentheses, commas in direct quotations, and apostrophes in the possessive case of nouns and in contractions.
- (+) 1.5 Use underlining, quotation marks, or italics to identify titles of documents.

Capitalization
- (+) 1.6 Capitalize names of magazines, newspapers, works of art, musical compositions, organizations, and the first words in quotations when appropriate.

Spelling
- (+) 1.7 Spell correctly roots, inflections, suffixes and prefixes, and syllable constructions.

Math, science, and social studies skills

- Preparation of reports and reference books
- Reading maps and globes
- Incorporating group problem solving and decision making
- Encouraging conclusions, inferences, generalizations
- Use of graphs

Resources and materials

- "One Inch Tall," *Where the Sidewalk Ends*, Shel Silverstein
- *Tom Thumb*
- *Issunboshi*, Robert B. Goodman/it. A. Spicer (core)
- *The Brocaded Slipper and Other Vietnamese Tales*, Lynette D. Vuong
- *The Emperor's Clothes*
- *The Magic Wings, A Tale from China*; D. Wolkstein
- *Rumpelstiltskin*
- *The Crane Wife*, K. Palerson (core)
- *National Geographic*, Japanese filmstrips
- *Tales from Around the World*, Jeanne Becijos, Dominie Press, 1991
- Picture file cards of the countries
- Two giant pop-up books of Momotaru
- *Children's Books*, Z. Sutherland
- *Best Found Folktales of the World*, J. Cole
- *Once Upon a Time—On the Nature of Fairy Tales*, Max Lilithi, translated by Chadeayne
- *In the Magic Corridor*, H. Eubanks, Dominie Press, 1990
- *Five Chinese Brothers*
- *Great, Big Enormous Turnip*
- *Stone Soup*
- *Why the Sun and the Moon Rise in the Sky*
- *Why Mosquitoes Buzz in People's Ears*
- *Toad Is the Uncle of Heaven*
- *Beyond the Hidden Door*, H. Eubanks, Dominie Press, 1991

Glad Unit Planning Pages
Comparative Folklore—Little People

Focusing and motivation

- Art activity: Thumbprint people
- Movie or filmstrip of folktale
- Artifacts, media, art prints from country represented
- Guest speaker about one of the countries
- Inquiry charts: What do you know about the country? What do you want to learn?
- Observation charts: Aspects of the culture or pictures from variations on the fairy tale
- World map
- Big Books
- Portfolios
- Students interview parents about folktales from their cultural background

Input

- Narrative input chart on folktale
- Read aloud—*Issunboshi* or selected tale over two days
  - Predicting charts (ongoing, daily processing), active participation, oral practice
- Same procedure for *Tom Thumb* and two or three other folktales that you are comparing
- Input chart on culture/customs of the time period (for example, ancient Japan for *Issunboshi*)
- Graphic organizer for three parts to the folktale, character traits, plot, differences from legends etc., ethical truths, or moral
- Poetry: "One Inch Tall"
- Story mapping

Guided oral practice

- Cooperative groups (group points): T-graph
- Personal interaction: Chip talking
  - Respond to the story.
    * Feelings: Have you ever been in a situation like Cinderella and felt unappreciated?
    * Interpretations: How do you think Issunboshi felt while playing with the children?
  - Discuss personal qualities of a hero.
- Process grid: Compare several versions of one tale or kinds of characters in several tales.
- Picture file cards: Find similarities in the artist's rendition of ancient Japan and the pictures of modern Japan. Come up with a group sentence. Use numbered-heads-together strategy to report team sentence.
- Group predictions: Share total class and record for Part Two on the chart.
- Group mind-mapping and webbing on specific topics
- Group poetry, chanting, and brainstorming changes in poetry frames
- Roundtable and list, group, label on hero/personality traits
- Mind mapping own thumbprint character
- Book-sharing circles
- Teams discuss good/evil and hero/villain.
- In teams, individuals share and dictate stories from their parents.

Reading and writing activities

- Total class modeling
  - Compare or contrast three aspects of heroes from different tales. Use the process grid to model structure.
  - Model highlighting, revising, editing.
  - Model group poetry or narrative frame.
  - Cooperative strip paragraph, expository: Compare and contrast

- Small group practice for scaffolding
  - Cooperative: Heterogeneous team tasks
    * Focused reading
    * Partner anticipation/prediction guide
    * Pairs of pairs: Each pair reads one part of the selection. Pairs return to cooperative group, share information, finish team worksheet. Quick whip to report answers.
    * Team mind-maps
    * Cooperative strip paragraphs: Each team, using their team mind-map, creates a paragraph. Each member writes a supporting detail after agreeing upon topic sentence.
    * Oral book sharing
    * Team plays, folktales, or puppet shows
    * Team poetry writing
    * Leveled reading group
    * ELD groupings
  - Individual choices
    * DEAR time
    * Personal exploration: Individuals can choose"TinyTales" (and write it in a tiny book), thumbprint illustrations and written text, original folktales, write and illustrate tale from parents, poems.
    * Interactive journals
    * Working logs, responding to the story, developing sentences from Farmer in the Dell chart or process grid.
    * Related nonfiction, such as Crass's biography of Tom Thumb; Charles Sherwood Straton, *Tom Thumb*; or modern fiction such as *The Borrowers* or *Stuart Little*.
    * Individual expository paragraph
  - Writers' workshop
    * Oral book-sharing discussions
    * Mini-lessons on focus, structure, voice, etc.
    * Peer conferencing on readings and writings
    * Conferences with teacher on writing

Extended activities for integration

- Role playing a folktale
- Folk songs to accompany folktales
- General background music from country, while writing
- Finger puppets
- Build dioramas for little people.
- Poetry from various countries
- Reader's theater
- Charades
- Graph favorite tales.
- Draw characters to put in windows of castle bulletin board.
- Dragon bookmarks
- Castle work spaces (witch can make characters appear or disappear for word problems)
- Poster advertising favorite tale
- Visualization (sketch and listen)

Closure

- Processing of all charts and learning
- Presentation of any team projects
- Presentation of personal exploration
- Have a teeny-tiny day. Do everything in miniature—use small balls for physical education, read only small books, make tiny sandwiches or tiny cookies, tiny cups, and tiny awards.
- Assessment conference with teacher. Student and teacher select the best materials from the unit portfolio to go in the permanent portfolio.
- Compare and contrast paragraph on two fairy tales from different countries.
- Sketch and write on elements of a fairy tale.

A Trip Around the World

At a transitional level, "A Trip Around the World" is intended as a study of cultures and communities within their geographical setting. It has been enlarged to include the study of a prominent ecosystem of each country or area. It takes two to three months to complete a unit of this size, so the in-depth comparative folklore is not included within the context of this unit. You may prefer to combine both units and put the plan on a four- to five-month megaunit. You could also extend the unit in physical science and have "Our World" as a year plan, rather than one unit. At a beginning ELD level, emphasis has been placed on the studies of the types of communities and their wants and needs or ecosystems. These lend themselves to high-interest studies of multicultural communities while using vocabulary and concepts crucial to beginning ELD students. The Living Wall centers around a *gigantic* world map.

Basic Outline of Trip

North America (Mexico)
Culture: Language
Community: Farming
Ecosystem: Farmlands
Writing: Narrative

South America (Brazil)
Culture: Tools
Community: Hunters/gatherers
Ecosystem: Rainforest/jungle
Writing: Analytical (cause and effect)

Africa
Culture: Religion/Beliefs
Community: Tribal
Ecosystem: Grasslands
Writing: Report of facts

Middle East
Culture: Art, holidays
Community: Nomadic
Ecosystem: Desert
Writing: Creating fictional characters

Europe
Culture: Rules/laws
Community: Cities (producers/consumers)
Ecosystem: Mountains
Writing: Biographies

Asia
Culture: Clothing/shelter
Community: Fishing/shipping
Ecosystem: Ocean
Writing: Persuasive

California
Culture: As a microcosm
Community: Many kinds
Ecosystem: Chaparral
Writing: Autobiography

GLAD Idea Page
Trip to North America (Mexico)

Subtheme—content

Our trip around the world begins with the study of Mexico, using geography, language, and the life of a farmer. Discuss the customs, culture, and experiences of any students from Mexican roots. Point out issues of immigration and prejudice.

Focusing and motivation (background information)

- Passports
- Inquiry charts
- Observation charts
- Music
- Slide show
- Finding Mexico on a wall map

Closure and evaluation

- Team big books
- Process charts/learning
- Share story of farmers

Concepts (Go to Frameworks and Standards)

- History and influence of Mexico on the United States (history/social science framework)
- Map skills
- Study of language as a function of culture
- The farmer as a chief producer of commodities
- The trolley as a vehicle of transportation

- Farmland ecosystem—what happens when the land can no longer support the people (Oklahoma and flight to California), comparing with droughts and lack of land and illegal immigration to the United states
- Issues of prejudice

Vocabulary (go to textbooks)

- Some Spanish vocabulary/cognates used in the United States that originated from Spanish:
  - Producer
  - Economy
  - Crops
  - Society
  - Drought
  - Ecosystem
  - Various farming terms
  - Clothing and food

English language arts skills (go to standards)

Choose as appropriate from overview. Skills will vary depending on grade level.

Math, social studies, and science

Choose as appropriate from overview. Skills will vary depending on grade level.

Resources and materials

- *Amigo*; Byrd, Baylor, 1987.
- *The Fall of the Aztecs*; Glubok, S., 1965.
- *Joel, Growing Up a Farm Man*; Denuth, P., 1982.

- *The Riddle of the Drum, A Tale from Lizapan*, Mexico; Aardema, V., 1960.
- "My Song Is a Piece of Jade," *Poems of Ancient Mexico*; ed. de Gerez, 1971.
- *Hill of Fire*; Lewis, T., 1971, 1983, 1987.
- *The Lady of Guadalupe*; De Paola, T., 1980.
- *Bridge Across the Americas*, Penny Cameron, Dominie Press, 1990.

GLAD Unit Planning Pages
Trip to North America (Mexico)

Focusing and motivation

- Trolley trip to Mexico
- Pass through customs and have passports stamped.
- Find Mexico on world map—start Living Wall.
- Inquiry charts
- Observation charts: Four areas of Mexican culture—shelter, business, art, transportation
- Interest pieces (students bring in newspaper and magazine articles): Become part of Living Wall.
- Background music and guided imagery of central plateau of Mexico; farming life

Input

- Pictorial map of Mexico: Introduce specific map skills.
- Narrative input chart: Life style of a farmer (what he produces, how he sells it, what and how he buys; comparison with farming in the United States)
- Pictorial input of a farmland ecosystem
- Laser discs

Guided oral practice (form cooperative groups with T-graph)

- Picture file cards: Draw conclusions.
- Team maps of Mexico
- Teams teach three to four words in Spanish.
- Personal interaction: Issue of drought, comparisons of farmers in the United States
- Mind maps of ecosystems
- Language wall
- Stereotyping activities
- Farmer in the Dell, sentence patterning chart
- Process grid
- Expert groups
- Team tasks

Reading and writing activities

- Total class: Group frame or cooperative strip paragraph format. Compare and contrast. Use signal words. Teach identified skills.
  - Poetry frame
- Small group practice: Flexible groupings
  - Cooperative activities
    * Book sharing
    * Cooperative strip paragraph
    * Ear-to-ear reading
    * ELD groupings
    * Team worksheet
    * Story mapping
    * Team tasks: anything that has been modeled by the teacher
    * Leveled reading groups
  - Individual activities
    * Personal exploration
    * DEAR time
    * Keep portfolio and atlas/encyclopedia.
    * Interactive journals or silent sustained writing

* Read with teacher from group frame or text for introduction, practice, and reinforcement of skills.
* Respond to content in learning logs.
- Required writing genre in teams and individually
  - Reading/Writing workshop to work on narrative piece
    * Reading and writing with partners or individually
    * Peer conferences about readings and writings
    * Author shares of quickshares and discussion of essential features and techniques
    * Mini-lessons on essential features, mapping, focus, voice, and audiences

Closure and evaluation

- Process charts
- Share individual narrative writing or personal exploration
- Discuss results of stereotyping
- Team and personal evaluations
- Portfolio assessment conferences with teacher
- Ongoing Learning Log assessment

GLAD Idea Page
Trip to South America

Subtheme: Content

The second leg of our trip is to the continent of South America. The study of Brazil and tribal cultures will include simple producer/consumer, communities of hunters/gatherers, and the study of tools. Guide students so that they can see that life in the rain forest is different than life in the cities of South America.

Focusing and motivation

- Passports/train (focusing background information)
- Inquiry charts
- Picture file of tools: Predict their use and justify prediction

Closure and evaluation

- Process charts and learning
- Oral presentation of tool
- Collecting folders
- Students write a descriptive paragraph of the rain forest

Concepts (go to frameworks and standards)

- Rainforest ecosystem
- Hunter/gatherer community
- Study of tools as a part of culture
- Vanishing jungles

Vocabulary (go to textbooks)

- Canopy
- Hunter/gatherer
- Slash and burn
- Producer/consumer
- Various animals/plants
- Tribal
- Rain forest
- Erosion
- Reseeding

Language arts, math, and science skills (go to standards)

Choose as appropriate from overview (writing domain: descriptive).

Resources

- Nonfiction
  - *Tropical Rain Forests: A Disappearing Treasure*; a pamphlet from the Smithsonian Institution.
  - *Lobo of the Tasaday: A Stone Age Boy Meets the Modern World*, Nance, J., 1982.
  - *National Geographic*: 4/87, 12/88, 9/87.
  - *Pele, The King of Soccer*; Gault, C., 1975.
  - *Picture Map Geography of South America*; Quinn, V., 1941.
  - *Brazil*; Jacobsen,K., 1989.
  - *Brazil*; Carpenter, A., 1987.
  - *Paulo of Brazil*; Cavanna, B., 1962.
  - *Brazil*; Cross, W., 1984.
  - *How People Live in Brazil*; Diericky, W., 1970.
  - *Getting to Know the River Amazon*; Joy, C., 1968.
  - *The Amazon*; McConnell, R., 1978.
  - *Ranger Rick*: "Nature Scope: The Rain Forest."
- Fiction
  - *The Jungle Book*; Kipling, R., 1984.
  - *The Just So Stories*; Kipling, R., 1987.
  - The Deer and the Jaguar Share a House
  - *Best Loved Folktales of the World*, ed., Cole, 1983.
  - *The Lorax*; Seuss, 1971.
  - *The Giving Tree*; Silverstein, S.
  - "The Five Brothers" (Chile), *Best Loved Folktales of the World*, ed. Cole, 1983.
- Texts
  - District science and reading texts

GLAD Unit Planning Pages
Trip to South America

Focusing and motivation (background information)

- Interest pieces
- Brainstorm
- Film about jungle: Ecosystem and community
- Everybody votes: Issues of disappearing jungle
- Guest speaker from World Wildlife Foundation

Input

- Narrative input, "Kim Plants a Seed": Tools that his parents and he use; their life style
- Comparative input: Kinds of tools
- Pictorial input: Ecosystem of jungle
- *National Geographic*: Read aloud

Guided oral practice (form cooperative groups)

- T-graph: Respect
- Debates on cause and effect of vanishing rain forest
- Picture file cards: Classify and categorize
- Language wall
- Chants and poetry
- Group discussion: Primitive tools, modern tools, future tools
- Use visualization: Jungle
- Process grid with expert groups: Start aspects of culture process grid.
- Farmer in the Dell, rain forests
- Personal interaction: The Vanishing Jungle
- Team flip chant

Reading and writing activities

- Total class modeling: Group frame/cooperative strip paragraph (teacher uses information from students to model appropriate frame and teach skills)
  - Frame format
    * Descriptive: A future tool; start with graphic organizer
    * Analysis: Cause and effect of vanishing jungle
- Reading and writing practice: Flexible groupings
  - Small group activities
    * Team graphic organizers
    * Roundtable: Jungle
    * ELD groupings
    * Expert groups on elements of the ecosystem
    * Draw and label team ecosystems.
    * Team tasks: team pictorial, team mind map, team farmer in the dell, team process grid, team paragraph, team story map
    * Ear-to-ear reading
    * Leveled reading groups
  - Individual activities
    * Personal exploration
    * Anything practiced by the group
    * Text reading: Read logs, cooperative strip paragraph, group frame, poetry booklet
    * DEAR time
    * Quick write
    * Interactive journals
- Keep portfolio and atlas/encyclopedia.
- Ongoing assessment with Learning Logs

Extended activities for integration

- Poetry, "I Know the Jungle": Frame
- Music of the area
- "The Important Book"
- Build a tool

- Song: "Where Have All the Jungles Gone?" (to the tune of "Where Have All the Flowers Gone?")
- Reader's theater: Jungle Book
- Graphing tools
- Sharing cooking and realia by parents
- Conte and water color art

Closure and evaluation

- Process all charts and learning.
- Oral presentation of student-invented tool and its uses
- Video
- Teaching and practicing of multiple-choice test
- Writing of a descriptive or analytical paragraph

Example of a narrative input frame

Part I

I want to tell you a story about Kim and his special tree. Kim lived in a beautiful tropical rain forest (jungle). His tribe lived far away from cities. Kim loved his jungle. He loved to see the wonderful animals and birds who lived in the trees of his forest. But most of all he loved playing and swinging through his beautiful trees. One day, as he was swinging through the trees he noticed a strange looking seed. He decided to plant it. First he found a place where not too many trees were around it because he knew trees needed sun and air. Second, he put it near a stream because he knew trees needed water. Third, he watched it for many days so that no animals or birds would dig it up.

Part II

Then one day, Kim noticed his tree came out from the ground. He looked very carefully and saw it was still connected to the seed. Kim knew he had to protect his seedling or animals might try to eat it. It grew fast in the warm, wet jungle and soon became a young tree called a sapling. Now birds began to nest in its branches, and

61

Kim often sat underneath and listened to them. A few fruit began to grow on the tree.

Part III

His tree grew and grew and soon became an adult and produced flowers and new seeds. Kim showed these seeds to his family who knew they were chocolate seeds. They would make chocolate or take the seeds to the market and sell them. Kim began to hear noises at the edges of his forest—loud noises, like a terrible monster. He didn't know what they were.

Part IV

One day as he came to the place where his tree should be, the terrible things were there, cutting down his tree and many others. They took the trees away on machines. They burned what was left on the floor of the jungle. Kim was very sad. That evening, after the people and machines left, Kim went to where his tree had been to say good-bye. He noticed they had forgotten something! One of the seeds from his tree. Kim picked up the seed lovingly and said, "My tree will never really die. I will replant it. Once again it will become a home for birds and animals!" He carried it far into the jungle and planted it—where it grows to this day . . . unless the machines have arrived.

Sample activity: Predicting a tool

Objective: Synthesis level of learned vocabulary

Focusing and motivation

1. Pass out picture cards of tools and discuss.
2. Close your eyes and picture a tool in your mind.
   - What does it look like?
   - What do you use it for?
   - Picture yourself using it.
   - Does it make your job easier?
3. Open your eyes and draw your tool.

4. Share.
5. Discuss what a tool is and how it can make a job easier.
   - Remember when we learned to guess at numbers (estimate)?
   - Today we will guess at—predict—what will happen to tools.

Input

1. In the olden days, what were tools like? Let's look at some. What are they used for? Are they easy to use or hard?
2. Let's look at some tools of today. How have they changed? Are they easier to use?
3. Let's look at some tools of the future, like Star Wars. Are they easier to use?
4. Now let's predict a future tool. For example, a carplane. Here is my idea (draw on chart). Let's make one together. Brainstorm ideas and pick one.
5. Now close your eyes and think of a tool that would make your job easier. Draw a picture of the tool and describe what it does. If you finish early, come and put these tools in their correct groups.

GLAD Idea Page
Trip to Africa

Subtheme: Content

Africa is a continent of many countries and cultures. Religion is one aspect of culture.

Focusing and motivation

- Boat trip/passports
- Large cookie/cake of Africa; eat your way through
- Picture file cards: Different countries of Africa

- Slides/video of grassland animals (video: Animals Are People, Too and The Gods Must Be Crazy)
- Visualization
- Observation charts: Various countries of Africa—Egypt, the Congo, South Africa, Ethiopia, Somalia, Ghana, Kenya

Closure activities

- Mural of grassland animals
- Puppet show/animals: Build puppets
- Process charts/learning
- Team books
- Written/oral reports on country in Africa
- Required writing

Concepts (go to frameworks and standards)

- Religion, values, and beliefs as an aspect of culture
- Tribal communities
- Grassland ecosystem
- Personal issue of prejudice in South Africa; prejudice in the United States; the slaves—when, why, and how
- Africa as a continent of varied countries: Egypt and Somalia

Vocabulary (go to textbooks)

- Grassland
- Ecosystem vocabulary
- Culture
- Religion
- Continent
- Country
- Prejudice
- Race

English language arts skills (go to ELA/ELD standards)

Choose as appropriate from overview (writing domain: Report of facts).

Math, social studies, and science

Choose as appropriate from overview.

Resources and materials

- Nonfiction
    - *National Geographic*, videos on grassland animals
    - *Animals Are People, Too* video
    - "Talking Drums of Africa," *Dancing Masks of Africa,* Price, C 1973.
    - *Jane Goodall: Living Chimp Style,* Fox, M., 1981.
- Fiction
    - *Jambo Means Hello*, Feelings, M., 1981.
    - *Moia Means One*, 1971.
    - *Plays from African Folktales* with ideas for acting, dance, costume, and music, Korty, C.
    - *The Crest and the Hide and Other African Stories*, Courlander, H. 1982.
    - *Mother Crocodile: An Uncle Amadon Tale from Senegal*, Guy, R. 1982.
    - *Bringing the Rain to Kapiti Plain*, Aardema, V., 1981.
    - *Why Mosquitoes Buzz in Peoples' Ears*: A West African Tale Aardema, V., 1975.
    - *Anansi the Spider*, McDermott, G., 1972.
    - *Beat the Story—Drum, Pum, Pum*, Bryan, A., 1987.

GLAD Unit Planning Pages
Trip to Africa

Focusing and motivation (background information)

- Interest pieces: Newspaper and magazine articles
- Boat trip with passports
- Slides of grasslands
- Video: *Animals Are People, Too* and *The Gods Must Be Crazy*
- Visualization: Sights and sounds of grasslands
- Inquiry charts/ Observation charts

Input

- Grassland ecosystem: Pictorial input
- Comparative input: Various countries and tribes
- Africa as a continent: Religions as a part of the communities; Africa has almost all beliefs
- Review of some countries in Africa
- Map skills
- Read aloud: Anansi stories

Guided oral practice (form cooperative groups)

- Personal interaction: Beliefs
- T-graph: Respect
- Picture file cards: categorize grassland and jungle; classify what part of the food chain
- Sharing in groups: Kinds of religions
- Process grid: Start kinds of communities grid
- "Farmer in the Dell" chant: Animals
- Compare with religions of Brazil's jungles
- Interest corners: Grassland animals

- Collecting folders
- Expert groups
- Poetry/chanting

Reading and writing activities

- Total class: Group frame/cooperative strip paragraph (teacher uses information from students to model appropriate frame)
  - Model mind map of facts (use process grid)
  - Group frame of one animal
  - Report of facts
- Reading and writing practice: Flexible groupings
  - Cooperative activities
    * Map of Africa: Mountains, rivers, countries
    * Venn diagram: Similarities and differences between and jungle grassland
    * Group art, oral and written report
    * Team tasks: anything previously modeled by teacher: poetry, input charts, brainstorms, farmer-in-the-dell charts, strip books, and so on
    * Flip chants on animals
    * Cooperative strip paragraphs
    * Team books
    * ELD groupings
  - Individual activities
    * DEAR time
    * Personal exploration
    * Learning logs
    * Portfolios
    * Interactive journals
    * Required paragraph: Report of facts
    * Personal adaptation of poetry

Extended activities for integration

- Poetry: "I Know the Grasslands" frame
- Cooking and realia shared by parents
- Songs: Folk songs from Africa
- Folktales: Anansi, the Spider
- Graphing kinds of animals
- Word problems: Work spaces with grassland animals
- Music and dance from Africa
- Water color art for grasslands

Closure and evaluation

- Process all charts and learning
- Team books or puppet show on grassland ecosystems
- Team and personal evaluations
- Ongoing learning logs
- Required paragraph and poem or chant

GLAD Idea Page
Trip to the Middle East

Subtheme: Content

The Middle East is a land of controversy. Its ancient history and various forms of art are studied from Egyptian, Persian, Mesopotamian (historical), and Islamic (modern) cultures.

Focusing and motivation

- Camel train/passports
- Visualization: Desert
- Art and artifacts from Middle East
- Collecting folders

- Observation charts
- Laser discs
- Guest speaker

Closure and evaluation

- Oral sharing of fictional character
- Processing charts and learning
- Assessment conference with teacher and student
- Ongoing assessment of learning logs
- Required paragraph
- Teaching of essay test format

Concepts (go to frameworks, standards)

- Nomad communities
- Holidays and art as a function of culture
- Desert ecosystem
- Ancient history

Vocabulary (go to textbooks)

- Islam
- Desert
- Nomad
- Moslem
- Irrigation
- Adaptation

Language arts skills (go to standards)

Skills will vary by grade level. Choose as appropriate from overview (writing domain: Creating a fictional character).

Math, social studies, and science

Choose as appropriate from overview.

Resources and materials

- Nonfiction
  - *Saudi Arabia in Pictures*, Gordon, E., 1979.
  - *The Bedouin*, Lancaster, F., 1978.
  - *Achmed, Boy of the Niger*, Russcoli, M.
  - *Iran*, Lengyel, E., 1981.
  - *They Lived Like This in Ancient Persia*, Neurath, M., 1970.
  - *The Middle East*, Abdallah, M., 1981.
  - *The Land and People of Afghanistan*, Clifford, M., 1989.
  - *The Tuareg—Nomads and Warriors of the Sahara*, Bleeker, 1964.
  - *The Desert Is Theirs*, Byrd, B., 1975.
  - *The Changing Desert*, Graham, A., 1981.
  - *Desert Dwellers*, Cuisin, M., 1987.
  - *Deserts*, Bailey, D., 1990.
  - *The Desert, What Lives There*, Bronin, A., 1972.
  - *Time Life: Desert*
- Fiction
  - *Aladdin and the Wonderful Lamp*, Lang, A., 1983.
  - *Sohrab and Rustum: A Persian Folktale*, retold, Chek, C. H.,1981.
  - *The Talking Parrot: A Pakistani Folktale*, retold, Chek, C. H., 1975.
  - *The Girl Who Loved the Wind*, Yolen, J., 1987.
  - "Ali Baba and the 40 Thieves," *Best Loved Folktales of the World*, ed., Cole, 1987.
  - "The Farmer and His Hired Help," *Best Loved Folktales of the World*, ed., Cole, 1987.
- Films

– Animals of the Desert
• Poetry and chants

Is This an Ecosystem?
(to the tune of "Did You Feed My Cow?" by Ella Jenkins)

Is this an ecosystem?   Yes, ma'am.
Is this an ecosystem?   Yes, ma'am.
Where is it placed?   It's in the desert.
Where is it placed?   It's in the desert.
Does it have six parts?   Yes, ma'am.
Can you tell me all?   Yes, ma'am.

Well, what is the first?   The sun, of course.
And what does it do?   Gives heat and light.
And what comes next?   Nonliving.
And what's nonliving?   It's never lived.
Give me some examples.   Water and sand.
And what comes third?   Producers.
And what are producers?   All the plants.
Give me some examples.   Bushes and cacti.
What do they do?   Give us food.

And what comes fourth?   Primary consumers.
And what are consumers?   Plant eaters.
Give me some examples.   Kangaroo rats.
What do they do?   They eat the plants.

And what comes fifth?   Secondary consumers.
And what are these?   Meat eaters.
Give me some examples?   Owl, fox.

71

GLAD Unit Planning Pages
Trip to the Middle East

Focusing and motivation (background information)

- Trip by camel train/passports
- Inquiry charts
- Guided imagery: Desert
- Pictures of art

Input

- Map input
- Nomad communities: Read aloud accounts of nomads (use map with the narrative).
- Culture: Customs, holidays, and art
- Desert ecosystem

Guided oral practice

- Expert groups: Six different nomad groups
- T-graph
- Presentations of life style: Oral brainstorming
- Process grid: Add to culture and community grids
- Desert island activity: Sharron Bassano (*Look Who's Talking*)
- Picture file cards: Observe and evaluate pictures of holidays and art
- "Farmer in the Dell" chant: Camels
- Flip chants
- Personal interaction: These deserts hold oil. Why? How does that affect us?

Reading and writing activities

- Total class/group frame: Create a fictional character.
  - Use mind map that shows real and fictional attributes.
- Reading and writing practice
  - Flexible groups
- Expert groups: Readings on nomad and desert groups
- Advance organizers such as anticipation and prediction guide
- Readings with learning logs
- Team strip books
- Leveled reading groups
- Guided reading from poetry booklet
  - Individual
    * DEAR time
    * Personal exploration
    * Interactive journals
    * Quickwrites: Learning logs and quickshares
    * Portfolios
    * Strip books

Extended activities for integration

- Change money
- Music for Middle East
- Work spaces
- Word problems
- Poetry from Khalil Gilbran and frames such as "I Know a Giant Lizard"
- Cooking and realia
- Examples of nonrepresentational art (no human portrayed)

Closure and evaluation

- Oral presentation of fictional character
  - Dress up
  - Monologue or dialogue sharing customs of character

- Processing learning/charts
- Model and practice multiple-answer test exam.
- Sketch and write everything you remember about the Middle East.

GLAD Idea Page
Trip to Europe

Unit theme

Like Africa, Europe is a continent of many countries, languages, governments, rules, and laws. Compare recent immigrants to the United States to early immigrants.

Focusing and motivation

- "Car trip" through Europe (done with pictures)
- Pictures of famous rulers, kings, etc.
- Inquiry chart on Europe/immigrants

Closure and evaluation

- Oral presentation of ruler's biography
- Biography and videotape presentations
- Process all charts and learning
- Individual required writing, presentations
- Utilize format for multiple-choice exam
- Teams' set of class "rules, laws, taxes, etc."
- Debate on whose rules will stand

Concepts (go to frameworks and standards)

- City communities (producer/consumer and goods/services)
- Rules and laws as a function of culture

- Mountain ecosystem
- Historical influence on United States
- Kings and queens in fact and fiction: Fairy tales versus biographies
- History is written with a certain perspective

Vocabulary (go to textbooks)

- Rulers (kings, queens, emperors, presidents)
- Governments
- Mountain ecosystem
- Rules and laws
- Consumer/producer society
- Goods/services society
- Biography
- Fact and fiction
- Folktales and fairy tales

Language arts skills

Skills will vary by grade level. Choose as appropriate from overview.

Math, social studies, and science skills

Choose as appropriate from overview.

Resources and materials

- Nonfiction
  - *Scandinavia*, Time Life, 1986.
  - *Welcome to Sweden*, Friskey, M., 1975.
  - *Sweden*, Hintz, M., 1985.
  - *Sweden, A Good Life for All*, Olsson, K., 1983.
- Fiction
  - *East of the Sun and West of the Moon and Other Tales,*

Asbjornson,P. and Jorgan, M., 1963.
- *Norse Gods and Giants*, D'Aulaire, 1986.
- *Shoemaker and the Elves*, Grimm, J. W., any version.
- *The Ugly Duckling,* Anderson, H. C., any version.
- *The Emperor's New Clothing*, Anderson, H. C., any version.
- *William Tell*, Bauden, N., 1989.
- *Pippi Longstocking,* Lindgren, A., 1981.
- *Pele's New Suit*, Beskow, E., 1929, 1979.
- *The King's Fifth*, O'Dell, S., 1966.
- *The Merry Adventures of Robin Hood*, Pyle, H., 1968.
- *The Nightingale*, Anderson, H. C., any version.
- *Queen Eleanor Independent Spirit*, Brooks, P., 1983.

GLAD Unit Planning Pages
Trip to Europe

Focusing and motivation (background information)

- Car trip/passports
- Pictures of kings, etc.: Famous rulers
- Read aloud
- Role play: Reader's theater from folktales
- Observation charts: Different countries

Input

- Travel shown on map: Map skills—Continue Living Wall
- City communities (consumer/producers; goods/services; jobs/ careers): Graphic organizers
- Cultural aspect: Picture file cards
- Mountain ecosystem
- Read aloud biography of famous ruler

Guided oral practice

- Act out various types of government as you discuss.
- Interest corners: Kind of government or ruler
- Picture file: Classify and categorize goods/services and producer/consumer.
- Process grid
- Numbered heads together processing
- Farmer in the Dell, sentence patterning chart
- Poetry and chanting
- Personal interaction
- Cooperative strategies

Reading and writing activities

- Total class: Group frame—Biography, model essential features
- Cooperative group/Flexible groupings
  - T-graph
  - Team tasks, labels mountain ecosystem
  - Team roundtables and list, group, label needs in governments
  - Team time lines for various people
  - Expert group information: Rules and governments of countries
  - Leveled reading groups
- Individual activities
  - DEAR time
  - Interactive journals
  - Learning logs
  - Portfolios
  - Personal exploration
  - Quickwrite: Biography frame
  - Write individual biographies (Encourage students to sit together by interest in countries or people.)
- Writing workshop: Mini-lessons
  - Model writing biography of famous European ruler that you have just read.
  - Model time lines and adapt writing to appropriate level. For

example, a first-grade student might write only two or three significant things. A fourth-grade student might write three paragraphs.

– Model turning time lines and mind maps into writing by making a cooperative strip paragraph frame.

Extended activities for integration

- Swedish poetry
- Integrating math activity
- Cooking and realia shared by parents
- Song, "Is This an Ecosystem?"
- Work spaces with word problems
- Role playing rulers: Reader's theater

Closure and evaluation

- Dress up as your ruler and present the biography of your person. Make a video.
- Process all charts and learning.
- Quickshare favorite piece in portfolio.
- Explain something in history from a different perspective.

Sample guided cooperative practice

Integrating math: Goods and services

Motivational set (Activate prior knowledge and review the pictures.)

- What do I know about goods and services?
- T-graph for social skills: Teacher graphs things seen and heard when students work cooperatively.

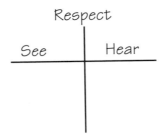

Guided cooperative practice

1. Form random groups for picture file activities.
   - Categorize goods and services.
   - Describe one good/service that you have bought or received this week.
   - Each group states results and how the group practiced respect.
2. Teacher introduces bar graph and sets criteria for success.
   - Graph must have six colors, title, and nearness.
   - Each group should be able to state, "We practiced respect by . . ." (stating two ways)
3. Teacher models and group follows.
   - Teacher models survey question. Students develop survey question.
   - Teacher models questioning and tallying. Students question and tally.
   - Teacher models making bar graph (using cut paper squares). Students make bar graph.

Closure

- Members of the group share
  - Bar graph
  - Two ways they met the criteria for success
  - Two ways they practiced respect

Possible survey questions

1. Which of these goods do you buy most often?
   ❑ ice cream ❑ hamburgers ❑ toys ❑ clothes

2. Which of these services do you use most often?
   ❑ TV repair ❑ teeth cleaning ❑ library services ❑ getting mail

3. When you grow up, would you rather sell goods or services?
   _____

4. Which of these community helpers would you like to be?
   ❑ doctor ❑ nurse ❑ dentist ❑ carpenter ❑ fireman

5. Which of these people who sell goods would you rather be?
   ❑ shoe salesperson ❑ food salesperson ❑ toy salesperson ❑ flower salesperson

6. Which uniform is the most interesting?
   ❑ policeman ❑ waitress ❑ astronaut ❑ doctor ❑ fireman

GLAD Idea Page
Trip to Asia

Unit theme

Asia is the largest and most populated continent. Discuss how the ocean has affected its growth. Discuss the various waves of immigration—their time periods and effect.

Focusing and motivation

- Fly/passports: Class goes to country of choice (interest corners).
- Map, pictures, and music of Asia
- Inquiry charts: Team or interest group inquiry charts

Closure and evaluation

- "Sell" your country. Write and present a travel advertisement.
- Process charts and learning
- Turn in portfolios
- Ongoing assessment with learning logs

Concepts (go to frameworks and standards)

- Asian communities: Fishing and shipping
- Houses and clothes as parts of culture
- Climate influences on houses and clothes
- Ocean ecosystem
- Personal issue: Fishing, polluting, water, or immigration and issues concerning prejudice and racism

Vocabulary (go to textbooks)

- Ocean ecosystem
- Shelter
- Clothing
- Customs
- Climate
- Pollution
- Extinction
- Endangered

Language arts skills (go to standards)

Choose as appropriate from overview (writing domain: persuasive).

Math, social studies, and science skills

Choose as appropriate from overview.

Resources and materials

- Fiction
  - *Magic Listening Cap*, Ichida, V., 1987.
  - *Umbrella and Crow Boy*, Yashima, T., 1977.
  - *Tales of a Korean Grandmother*, Carpenter, F., 1972.
  - *Momotaro*, Motomora, M., 1989.
  - *Doi Song Moi, A New Life in a New Land*, Hien, W., 1989.
  - *Yeh-Shin, A Chinese Cinderella*, Louie, A., 1988.
  - *Beyond the East Wind: Legends and Folktales of Vietnam*
  - *Chinese Mother Goose Rhymes*, Weyndham, R., 1989.
  - *The Crane Wife*, Yagawa, S., 1981.
  - *Mom's Kitten*, Yashima, M. and Y., 1977.
  - *Vietnamese Legends*, Hap, D. H.
  - *Angel Child, Dragon Child*, Surat, M., 1983.
  - *Sea of Gold and Other Tales from Japan*, Yamaguchi, M., 1988
  - *Toad Is the Uncle of Heaven*, Lee, J., 1985.
  - *Two Brothers and Their Magic Gourds*, Adams, E., 1981.
  - *Eyes of the Dragon*, Leaf, M., 1987.
  - *Perfect Crane*, Laurin, A., 1987.
- Nonfiction
  - *The Weaving of a Dream*, Heyer, M., 1986.
  - *Look What We've Brought You From Vietnam*, Shalant, P., 1988.
  - *Six Centuries in East Asia, China, Japan and Korea*, Lum, P., 1987.
  - *The Aftermath: Asia*, Time Life.
  - *Taiwan: Island China*, Cooke, D.
  - *South Korea*, Lye, K., 1985.
  - *Korea*, McNair, S., 1986.
  - *Welcome to Japan*, Friskey, M., 1975.
  - *National Geographics*
  - Embassies and consulates

GLAD Unit Planning Pages
Trip to Asia

Motivation

- Interest pieces: Daily news
- Fly with passports: Groups to each country (different interest corners)
- Inquiry charts: Cooperative groups
- Guest speaker
- Observation charts

Input

- Ocean communities: Fishing and shipping; a study of housing, clothes, climates, and cultures
- Comparative input: Japan, Taiwan, Vietnam
- Ecosystem of ocean life: Add to Living Wall.
- Map skills: Where various countries are

Guided oral practice

- Picture file cards: Draw conclusions; compare and contrast; housing, clothes, and weather
- Expert groups: Experts of chosen country
- Numbered heads together
- Process grid
- Team tasks
- Personal interaction: Pollution, overfishing the seas, issues of
- Prejudice and stereotypes
- "Farmer in the Dell" chant: Fish

Reading and writing activities

- Total class: Group frame or cooperative strip paragraph
  - Persuasion: Write a travel brochure.
  - Prewrite, discuss, and create poster.
- Cooperative/Small group/Flexible groups
  - Expert groups: Country
  - Mind maps of country information
  - Group travel poster, brochure, and advertisement for visiting a country
  - Read-arounds: Revise and edit.
  - Ear-to-ear reading with anticipation or prediction guide
  - Comparative folktales
  - Flexible group reading
  - ELD groupings
- Individual
  - DEAR time
  - Silent sustained writing: Writer's workshop
  - Interactive journals
  - Personal exploration
  - Read with learning logs
  - Quickwrite and quickshares
  - Required writing to persuade

Extended activities for integration

- Song: "Listen to the Water," by Bob Schneider
- Cooking and realia from various countries
- Folk songs from countries
- Guided imagery: The ocean
- Hyperstudio

Closure and evaluation

- Share and hang up posters, present brochures, "sell" your country.

- Process charts and learning.
- Before and after graph: Vote on which country you would like to visit and why.
- Write poetry or chant.
- Students fill in process grid for assessment.

GLAD Idea Page
Returning Home (California)*

Unit theme

California is a microcosm of the world. Compare aspects of communities, cultures, and ecosystems.

Focusing and motivation

- Fly/passports /customs
- Inquiry charts
- Map of California

Closure and evaluation

- Cultural museum
- Big Books
- Process comparing all charts and process grids
- Discussion groups of personal discoveries and growth
- Sketch and write comparing cultures
- Presentation on one's own roots

---

*This model uses California as "home," but the activities can be applied to any state.

Concepts (go to frameworks and standards)

- California is a cultural microcosm of the world.
- California contains many kinds of communities.
- California has a unique ecosystem: Chaparral.
- Personal issue: Cause and effect of immigration
- Research into our own roots

Vocabulary (go to textbooks)

- Review cultural vocabulary (institutions, beliefs, etc.).
- Review community vocabulary (consumer/producer, etc.).
- Review ecosystem vocabulary (primary producer, etc.).

Language arts skills

Choose as appropriate from overview (writing domain: autobiography).

Math, social studies, and science skills

Choose as appropriate from overview.

Resources and materials

- *The Earth Is Our Mother*, Eargle, D., 1989.
- *Keepers of the Earth*, Caduto, M., 1988.
- *Ishi, Last of His Tribe*, Kroeber, 1964.
- *Island of the Blue Dolphins*, O'Dell, S., 1987.
- *Conquista!*, Bulla, C. and Syson, M., 1978.
- *The King's Fifth (reminiscences of a 15-year-old cartographer to Coronado)*, O'Dell, S., 1966.
- *The Year of the Boar and Jackie Robinson*, Lord, B., 1984.
- *How My Parents Learned to Eat*, Friedman, I.
- *Men to Match My Mountains*, Stone, I., 1987, or other stories about crossing the Sierras.

GLAD Unit Planning Pages
Returning Home (California)

Focusing and motivation

- Fly/passports
- Inquiry charts
- Map of California
- Graph of ethnic background of class
- Read aloud: Autobiography of Californians

Input

- Comparative
  - California is a microcosm of the world culturally: Use comparative cultures process grid.
  - California contains many types of communities: Use comparative input charts.
- Pictorial
  - California has a unique environment: Chaparral ecosystem.
- Read autobiography of Californians.
- Time line

Guided oral practice

- Comparative ecosystems activity (see background information)
- Process grid
- "Farmer in the Dell" chant: Californians
- Interview parents and relatives
- Expert groups
- Team tasks

Reading and writing activities

- Total class/group frame or cooperative strip paragraph
  - Autobiography
- Flexible groupings
  - Team tasks: Team expository paragraph, chant, narrative
  - Leveled reading groups
  - ELD groups
  - Expert groups
- Individual choices
  - Quickwrites
  - DEAR time
  - Portfolios
  - Text reading
  - Personal exploration
  - Interactive journals
- Writer's workshop
  - Write your autobiography
  - Mini-lessons
    * Model personal time lines and pick one significant incident.
    * Model group frame of writing an autobiographical incident (as appropriate to grade level).
    * Model highlighting for revising.
  - Peer conferences and teacher conferences on autobiographies

Extended activities for integration

- Poetry: "Earth Songs," Myra Cohen Livingston
- Graph
- Share Native American realia and food.
- Create a California cultural museum with realia from everyone. Students train as docents and parents tour.

Closure and evaluation

- Big Book of country of choice or one aspect of a country
- Create a country of your own. Meet rubric created by teacher and class.
- Final essay/report comparing and contrasting two continents

Life in a Pond

"Life in a Pond" began as a unit to develop reading vocabulary and concepts for a basal primer so that beginning students would understand the necessary vocabulary to make sense, or as much sense as is possible, from the primer. The unit revolves around a pond, the various life forms in and around it, the water and weather cycle, and conservation. It is primarily a science unit and fun to do in the spring when hands-on activities can include tadpoles turning into frogs and silkworms into moths. This unit was of high interest to our beginning students who acquired a phenomenal amount of English when discussing fascinating science ideas and wonderful animals. With logs of hands-on activities and experiments, which allowed for great total physical response (TPR) lessons, class discussion truly focused on the message and not the form.

At the end of this unit, with lots of chanting, discussions, and experiments, reading from the text becomes simple and only an aside for the children because it does not contain information as interesting as what they have learned. The children acquire enough vocabulary orally and in print that they are immediately successful when reading from the reading primer and the woefully inadequate science text.

At a transitional, or SDAIE, level, "Life in a Pond" has become one of the favorite units of our transitional or regular teachers. The opportunities for hands-on activities and oral discussion allow for "high ceiling/low-floor" teaching. All students are involved, can contribute, and stay motivated. Students check books out from the library and insist on teachers and parents reading them. They sketch scientific examples of bugs and critters and label them. They write about them and build models, terrarium, and aquariums.

GLAD Idea Page
Life in a Pond

Unit theme

"Life in a Pond" encompasses the life, physical, and earth sciences surrounding a pond. Subunits comprise water, reptiles, amphibians, insects, birds, fish, green plants, and the interdependence of life.

Focusing and motivation

- *Small Worlds of Life,* National Geographic filmstrip: Turn off sound and add your own narration.
- Daily read aloud, relevant to each subunit
- Start pond terrarium
- Movie: *Life in a Pond*
- Real animals and other items
- Inquiry charts
- Go to a pond. Have lunch at a pond. Make children responsible for written or sketched observations of a pond.
- Pond portfolios
- Start Living Wall: Huge pond and surroundings

Closure and evaluation

- Projects
  - Diorama
  - Make fish skeleton.
  - Art of fish bowls (wax paper, crayon shavings)
  - Fantastic fish awards
  - Create a terrarium.
  - Share projects, Big Books, work.

- Process charts and learning.
- Assessment: Teacher and student pick five best pieces from portfolio, conference, and add to permanent portfolio.
- Various forms of assessment are taught and practiced.

Concepts (go to frameworks and standards for grade level)

- Life cycles of animals, plants, and ponds
- Interdependence of life
- Water as a solid, liquid, and gas: Water cycle
- Characteristics of animal and plant groups
- Compare and contrast groups.

Vocabulary (go to the textbook)

- Differs for each subunit

Oral language, reading, and writing skills (go to ELA and ELD standards)

These will differ for each subunit and grade level taught. This is a summary of emerging literacy skills that can cross grade levels for beginning readers. The following list is incomplete, and not all these skills should be taught to all classrooms within this unit.
- Reading
  - Decoding
    * Sight words
    * Initial/ending consonants and sounds
    * Word families
    * Contextual clues
  - Comprehension
    * Sequence
    * Main idea
    * Drawing conclusions

- * Specific details
- * Cause and effect
- * Inferential
- * Organizing and categorizing information
- * Accessing, focusing background information
- * Fact/opinion and fiction/nonfiction
  - − Oral reading
    - * Fluency
    - * Interpretation
  - − Literature
    - * Variety of literary types: Fiction, nonfiction, poetry, etc.
  - − Study skills
    - * Parts of a book
    - * Alphabet
    - * Dictionary and encyclopedia (recognition, some use)
    - * Self-questions
    - * Beginning test-taking skills
    - * Organizing, categorizing
- Language arts
  - − Expressive, oral
    - * Expresses views, opinions in group
    - * Reports of information
    - * Respects views of others
    - * Observing and describing pictures, events
  - − Receptive
    - * Reacts to questions
    - * Follows directions
    - * Critical listening
    - * Knows purpose and draws conclusions
  - − Written expression
    - * Brainstorming, mind map
    - * Drafting, writing both free choice and frames
    - * Revising and editing for specific purpose and in appropriate place in writing process
  - − Grammar/usage
    - * Adjectives

* Statements and questions
* Pronouns
* Verbs: Present, past, future, and past participle
- Mechanics
  * Beginning and ending sentence: Capital letters and punctuation
  * Question marks, exclamations
  * Titles
  * Dates
  * Abbreviations

Math, science, and social studies skills

Each subunit will differ as will the grade level appropriateness. The following summary is not intended to be all inclusive.
- Information and research skills
  - Tests: Beginning skills and lowering of anxiety
  - Organize information.
  - Create a product, recognizing process
  - Parts of a book: Texts and references, titles, table of contents
  - Analyze data: Order and classify
  - Time: Chronology and time lines
  - Use of and ability to read graphs, charts, and so on
- Thinking and problem-solving skills
  - Use of processes for problem solving in group and individually
  - Critical thinking: Justify positions
  - Similarities and differences: Categorize information, predict
  - Outcomes, cause and effect sequence, conclusions
  - Know that there are often several ways to solve a problem.
  - Recognize and value individual and cultural differences.
- Science
  - Use diagrams and illustrations.
  - Thinking and problem-solving skills as above
  - Observe and record observations, inferring.
  - Apply information.

- Math
  - Three-dimensional shapes: Containers
  - Number concepts: Addition, subtraction, and word problems (done on workspaces)

Resources and materials

- Listed under individual subunits

GLAD Unit Planning Pages
Life in a Pond: Water

Focusing and motivation

- Inquiry charts: What do you know about water? Written on chart paper, read, and processed daily
- Super hydrologists' awards
- Observation charts: Sources and uses of water

Input

- Experiment: Water changes. How does water get into ponds? Melt ice cubes to water, then to steam. Put metal cover above steam and observe condensation. Observe and chart changes.
- Pictorial input chart of water cycle—10/2 lecture. Add to Living Wall.
- Experiment on pollution: Collect water from a pond, a puddle, and tap water. Leave to dry up. Observe and chart what remains.
- Experiment: Water takes the shape of its container. Pour water into different-shaped containers. Freeze and observe how its form, but not its shape, changed.
- Record hypotheses and results on charts and graphs.
- Tree of Life: Classification graphic organizer

Guided oral practice

- Form cooperative groups: T-graph on cooperation (as scientists)
- Farmer in the Dell: Scientists take to reading flip chant
- Process grid
- Teams form hypotheses, discuss results, and draw a chart showing changes.
- Teams predict which water will be the most polluted.
- Teams estimate which container will hold the most water.
- Teams draw and share with the class a water cycle.
- Personal interaction: What can we do about pollution?
- Team develops strip book.
- Choral reading, songs

Extended activities for integration

- Individual picture, water color art
- Create antipollution posters.
- Take pollution trip around school or a pond: Collect and throw away trash.
- Make pollution collage.
- Directed art lesson for Big Book
- Workspaces centered around pollution
- Poetry and chanting

Reading and writing activities

- Total class
  - Chart group frame or cooperative strip paragraph using information from students, for factual report: Water has three forms.
  - Paragraph is revised and edited, then typed and each student has copy in log. It is used for reading practice and reinforcement of reading skills.

- Small group/cooperative/leveled
  - Flexible
    * Oral book sharing
    * Partner reading
    * Ear-to-ear reading
    * Team tasks: Team mind maps, strip books, flip chants
    * Peer conferencing
    * Pairs of pairs reading with team worksheet
    * Team Big Books
    * Small group/large group mini-lessons by teacher on needs and skills observed in conferencing
    * Leveled reading groups
    * Expert groups: heterogeneous groups
    * ELD/SDAIE groups
  - Individual
    * DEAR time
    * Interactive journals
    * Text reading with responses in logs
    * Personal exploration
    * Reading/writing workshop
  - Mini-lesson
  - Author's chair

GLAD Idea Page
Life in a Pond: Fish

Fish have many different characteristics. How are they the same or different from humans? What is the cultural importance of fish around the world? Fish can be found in both fact and fiction.

Focusing and motivation

- Real fish, bones, fossils
- Inquiry charts about fish
- Read aloud: Both nonfiction and fiction about fish
- National Geographic video on fish

Closure and evaluation

- Share fish projects or reports.
- Share personal explorations.
- Process all charts and learning.
- Eat seaweed and dried Japanese squid.
- Student and teacher conference to select pieces for permanent portfolio
- Sketch and write comparing fish.

Concepts (go to frameworks and standards)

- Parts of a fish: Gills, fins, backbone, scales
- Life cycle and characteristics of fish
- Food chain: What do they eat and what eats them? The biggest animals (whales) do not eat the biggest fish.
- Fresh versus salty water
- Cultural aspects of fish around the world
- Fish in fiction from around the world

Vocabulary (go to textbooks)

- Gills
- Fins
- Backbones
- Hatch
- Cold-blooded
- Scales
- Salt water
- Schools
- Food chain

Oral language, reading, and writing skills (go to ELA and ELD standards)

Choose as appropriate from overview.

Math, science, and social studies skills (go to standards)

Choose as appropriate from overview.

Resources and materials

- Nonfiction
  - *National Geographic*: 6/88, 5/88, 4/75, 4/73.
  - *A Closer Look at Fish*, Banister, K., 1980.
  - *Fishes*, Fichter, G., 1963.
  - *Barracuda*, Jacobs, F., 1981.
  - *Sea Horse*, Stephens, W., 1964.
  - *Salmon*, Hogan, P., 1984.
  - *Sharks*, Blumburg, R., 1976.
  - *Sharks and Troubled Water*, Harris, M., 1977.
  - *The Long Lost Coelacanth*, Aliki, 1973.
  - *Animal Life*, Brimax.
  - *About the Biggest Salmon*, Hayes, W., 1961.
  - Marine Education Program (Los Angeles City Schools).
  - "Sharks," *Zoobooks*.
  - Ranger Rick, 2/84.
  - *Fish Do the Strangest Things*, Hornblow, L. and A., 1966.
- Fiction
  - *Sea Horse*, Morris, R., 1972.
  - *Fish Out of School*, Shaw, E., 1970.
  - *Swimmy*, Lionni, L., 1973.
- Folktales
  - *King of the Fishes*, Jacob, J.
  - *Little Mermaid*, Anderson, H. C., any version.
  - *King of the Fish*, Parry, M., 1977.
  - *Greyling*, Yolen, J., 1968.
  - *The Mermaid of Zennor*, Cornish tale.
  - *The Fisherman*, Aesop (core), any version.
  - *Yeh-Shen*, Chinese tale (core).
  - *Sea Hare*, Grimms, any version.
  - *The Fisherman and His Wife*, Grimms, any version.

- Poetry
  - "*Where the Sidewalk Ends*," Silverstein, S. (core), 1974.
  - "*Light in the Attic*," Silverstein, S. (core), 1981.
  - "*Cricket Songs*," Behn, H., 1964.
  - "*Piping Down the Valleys Wild*," Larrick, N. (core), 1982.
  - Poetry frames: "*Fish Here, Fish There*" (See Chapter 5, Strategies and Terms.)

GLAD Unit Planning Pages
Life in a Pond: Fish

Focusing and motivation

- Inquiry charts by cooperative groups: What do you know, and what do you want to learn? Make up five challenge questions for another team.
- Fish realia: Skeletons, eels, and so on
- Fish filmstrip: National Geographic
- Interest pieces about fish
- Portfolios

Input

- Experiment: Get anchovies from bait store; have teams observe and dissect. (You can dissect anchovies with toothpicks; you don't need knives.) Teacher guides about characteristics—teeth or the lack thereof and what that means about diet; tail shape and what that means about speed; coloring and what that means about protection.
- Pictorial input chart: Parts of a bony fish
- Tree of Life graphic organizer on kinds of fish and where it fits into other animal families: Add to Living Wall.
- Comparative input chart: Bony fish, cartilaginous fish, and jawless fish (kids love the jawless fish)
- Narrative input: Life cycle of fish, using *Sea Horse* by Morris as a basis

Guided oral practice

- Form cooperative groups with T-graph: Team work
- Pick a team fish, draw it, label it, research its characteristics, share. Team Exploration Reports
- Picture file: Classify, categorize, find examples of characteristics.
- "Farmer in the Dell" chart
- Process grid: Kinds of fish
- Personal interaction: Personal experiences or feelings about fish, issues of overfishing
- Choral reading of walls, charts, and poetry
- Poetry and chanting
- Team tasks

Reading and writing activities

- Total class
  - Expository: Facts or comparing/contrasting
  - Folktale: Story Map and Narrative
- Cooperative/flexible groupings
  - Team tasks mind maps, cooperative strip paragraphs, reports on fish, team flip chants, strip books (rewriting of frames, or make original)
  - Ear-to-ear reading with anticipation and prediction guide
  - Partner reading, individual reading
  - Story mapping
  - Peer conferencing
  - Expert groups (texts and references)
  - Leveled reading groups
  - ELD and SDAIE groupings
- Individual choices
  - Personal exploration: Expository, narrative, poetry, drama, art, diorama, etc.
  - DEAR time
  - Interactive journals

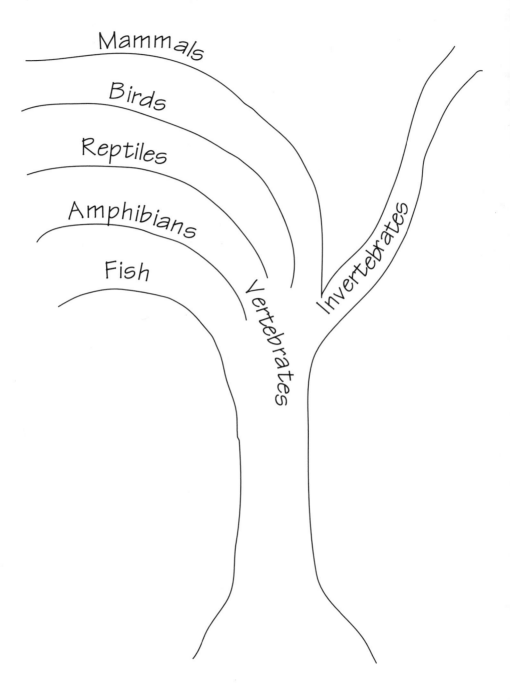

– Narrative: Rewrite or develop original.
– Student and teacher conferences: Both ongoing and final to pull best pieces
- Reading/writing workshop
  – Mini-lesson
  – Author's chair

Extended activities for integration

- Poetry
- Fish food chain mobile
- Clay prints: Fossil (like the coelacanth)
- Brayer fish art and labeling
- Fish songs
- Crayon resist, water color wash with marking pen
- Tissue paper with marking pens
- Pepperidge Farms goldfish crackers for use with work space and word problem
- Wax paper fish bowl with cutouts of fish, glitter and crayon shavings
- Water color crayons for directed art lesson for Big Book

Closure and evaluation

- Eat seaweed, dried Japanese squid.
- Share Big Books and projects.
- Process all charts and learning.
- Share personal explorations.
- Portfolio assessment conferences

GLAD Idea Page
Life in a Pond: Water birds

Unit theme

Life cycles and characteristics of water birds. Birds are being endangered around the world. Water birds have specific attributes.

Focusing and motivation

- Inquiry charts
- Film: *Water Birds* and *Petey the Pelican*
- Ornithologist awards
- Collecting folders
- Observation charts of birds

Closure and evaluation

- Projects
- Process charts and learning
- Portfolio assessment conferences

Concepts (go to frameworks and standards)

- Life cycles
- Characteristics: Waterproof feathers, live on or near water, usually get food from water, webbed feet, down feathers under contour feathers, hollow bones, homes usually low to the ground
- Water versus air birds

Vocabulary (go to textbooks)

- Waterproof
- Webbed

- Down feathers
- Hatch
- Beak/bill
- Hollow bones
- Molt
- Migrate
- Contour feathers

English language arts skills (go to ELA and ELD standards)

Choose as appropriate from overview.

Math, science, and social studies skills

Choose as appropriate from overview.

Resources and materials

- Basal and science texts
- Films
  - *Birds in Your Backyard*
  - *Birds: How They Live, Where They Live*
  - *Petey the Pelican*
  - *Water Birds*
  - *Alphabet of Birds*
  - *Where the Pelican Makes Her Nest*
  - *Adventures of a Young Eagle*
- Fiction
  - *Seabird*, Holling, H. C., 1975.
  - *The Crane Wife*, Yagawa, S., 1987.
  - *Sadako and the Thousand Paper Cranes*, Coerr, 1997.
  - *The Golden Goose*, ed. Cole, 1985.
  - *The Goose with the Golden Eggs*, ed. Cole, Grimm or any version.

- Nonfiction
  - *National Geographic*
  - "*The Man Who Painted Birds*," HBJ Reading Texts, 2nd grade.
  - *Zoobooks*, San Diego Zoological Society
  - *Ranger Rick*: "Nature Scope"

GLAD Unit Planning Pages
Life in a Pond: Water Birds

Focusing and motivation

- Inquiry charts
- Film: *Petey the Pelican* and *Where the Pelican Builds Her Nest*
- Ornithologist awards
- Read aloud: *Ranger Rick*
- Collecting folders

Input

- Experiment with feathers: Waterproofing and the way they fit together, preening—rub the feathers the wrong way and the barbules will not stick together. The opposite is also true. Water beads up.
- Pictorial input chart: A water bird—Add to Living Wall.
- Narrative input: Life cycle, characteristics, what they eat and what eats them
- Read aloud: *A Duckling Is Born*
- Graphic organizer: Fresh versus salt-water birds and names of various kinds

Guided oral practice

- Form cooperative groups with T-graph: Take turns.
- Teams pick a bird, draw it, and label the parts.

- Picture file: Categorize and classify
- Numbered heads together for reporting
- Class or team graphic organizers or mind maps
- "Farmer in the Del" chart
- Process grid
- Game: "I'm thinking of a bird that has . . ."
- Poetry and chanting: "I Am a Pelican," choral reading
- Expert groups, research, share and use numbered heads together to fill in process grid.
- Reading the walls with a partner
- Personal interaction: Effects of DDT

Reading and writing activities

- Total class
  - Expository: Compare and contrast birds.
  - Poetry frame
  - Sequential or narrative frame
- Cooperative/small group
  - Ear-to-ear reading with pairs of pairs, team comes back to fill in one worksheet
  - Partner reading
  - Peer conferences
  - Team expository frame using cooperative strip paragraph
  - Oral book sharing
  - Teacher gives class or group mini-lessons
  - Shared book experiences
  - Leveled reading groups
  - ELD and SDAIE groups
- Individual
  - Self-selected readings and writings on topic
  - Flip chant or strip book
  - Interactive journals
  - DEAR time
  - Personal exploration

- Student and teacher conferences
- Required writings
- Reading/writing workshop
  - Mini-lesson
  - Author's chair

Extended activities for integration

- Poem: "Jack Prelutsky," Random House, pp. 83–86.
- Collecting folders
- Papier-mache birds
- Mother/child books
- Work spaces: Can use a pond or a nest
- Graph birds most often seen.
- Visualization: Flight
- Listen and Sketch

Closure and evaluation

- Projects: To teacher and class developed rubrics
- Process charts and learning.
- Share Big Books.
- Share personal experiences.
- Portfolio assessment conferences.
- Students fill in process grids for assessment.

GLAD Idea Page
Life in a Pond: Reptiles

Unit theme

Life cycles, characteristics. Reptiles are present in most regions of the world. Humans have different attitudes toward reptiles.

Focusing and motivation

- Inquiry charts in groups
- Live reptiles
- Herpatologist awards
- Field trip to turtle farm or zoo

Closure and evaluation

- Build a terrarium or make a pet rock.
- Share personal experiences.
- Process charts and learning.
- Portfolio assessment conferences
- Ongoing learning log assessment

Concepts (go to frameworks and standards)

- Reptiles are cold-blooded, have scales, are not good parents after their eggs hatch, are born from eggs, have leathery (not slimy) skin and spines.
- There are five groups of reptiles: turtles, lizards, snakes, crocodilians, tuataras, and one extinct form—the dinosaur.
- Reptiles are present in many regions of the world.

Vocabulary (go to textbooks)

- Cold-blooded
- Leathery
- Hatch
- Iguana and other specific names
- Spines
- Scales

English language arts skills (go to ELA and ELD standards)

Choose as appropriate from overview.

Math, science, and social studies skills

Choose as appropriate from overview.

Resources and materials

- Nonfiction
  - *Snakes and Other Reptiles*, Elting, M., 1987.
  - *Snapping Turtles*, May, J., 1972.
  - *Alligators*, Shaw, E., 1972.
  - *National Geographic*
  - *Reptiles Do the Strangest Things*, Hornblow, L., 1970.
  - *Zoobooks*: "Turtles," "Snakes," and "Crocodiles"
  - *The Remarkable Chameleon*, Hess, L., 1968.
  - *Ranger Rick*: "Red Racer" and "How I Know Turtles"
- Fiction
  - *Lyle, Lyle, the Crocodile*, Weber, B., 1987.
  - *Brontosaurus Moves In*, Choose Your Own Adventure.
  - *Lizard's Song*, Shannon, G., 1981.
  - *The Fisherman and the Grateful Turtle*, Taro, U., 1985.
- Poetry
  - *Where the Sidewalk Ends*, Silverstein, S., 1974.
  - *New Kid on the Block*, Prelutsky, J., 1984.
  - *Talking to the Sun*, Metropolitan Museum, 1985.
  - *Alligator Pie*, Lee, D.

GLAD Unit Planning Pages
Life in a Pond: Reptiles

Focusing and motivation

- Inquiry charts: Daily reading and processing
- Live reptiles: Observe and handle
- Herpetologist awards
- Read aloud: Reptiles Do the Strangest Things
- Add to Living Wall

Input

- Comparative input chart: Turtles/tortoises
- Graphic organizers: Crocodilians
- Mind map: Snakes
- Narrative input: Lizards at the zoo—protective adaptation
- Poetry frames: "I Know a Giant Lizard," "Snakes Here, Snakes There"
- Big Book: "Reptiles are . . ." based on Quick as a Cricket
- Use of metaphors, descriptive language

Guided oral practice

- Form cooperative groups: T-graph for sharing
- Class and team mind maps: "Guess my rule for organizing class mind map."
- "Farmer in the Dell" chant: Reptiles
- Picture file activities
  - Classifying
  - Comparing
  - Observing characteristics
  - Making hypotheses
- Strip books

- Numbered heads together for the process grid
- Flip chants
- Poetry and chanting
- Personal interaction: Why are people afraid of reptiles? Are you?

Reading and writing activities

- Total class
  - Expository frame: Snakes are unusual in many ways.
  - Poetry frame: "Snakes Here, Snakes There"
  - Descriptive frame: Reptiles are . . .
- Small group/ flexible groupings
  - Cooperative
    * Sentences made and read by teams with word cards from "Farmer in the Dell" chart
    * Team tasks
    * Team flip chants or strip books
    * Team Big Book
    * Team crosswords and treasure hunts
  - Peer conferencing on readings and writings
    * Group mini-lessons by teacher
    * Partner reading, focused reading
    * Shared book experience
    * Reading practice from group frame—leveled groups
- Individual choices
  - Personal exploration
  - Interactive journals
  - DEAR time
  - Individual mind maps and organizers
  - Readings from texts and response in logs
  - Self-selected reading with teacher conferences
- Reading/writing workshop
  - Mini-lesson
  - Author's chair

Graphic Organizer: Crocodilians

Crocodiles   Alligators   Gharials

Crocodilians

Extended activities for integration

- Directed art lesson of mosaic art
- Iguana song: "I Want an Iguana," Sesame Street
- Poetry: Frames and "Alligators Are Unfriendly," Silverstein.
- Acting out narrative input and other readings
- Poetry/chanting/movement
- Listen and sketch

Closure and evaluation

- Share personal explorations, Big Books.
- Process all charts and learning.
- Process T-graph for behaviors.
- Portfolio assessment conferences

GLAD Idea Page
Life in a Pond: Insects

Unit theme

Insects make their homes all over the world. Some help us, such as the silkworm of China; some hurt us by carrying diseases. Insects are important in the tree of life. We all have our own personal view of insects and why we feel that way.

Focusing and motivation

- Silkworms
- Ant farms
- Real honeycombs
- Inquiry charts: What do we know about insects? What do we want to learn?
- Film
- Observation charts

Closure and evaluation

- Collecting folders
- Pancakes with honey
- Portfolio assessment conferences
- Ongoing assessment with learning logs
- Practice and utilization of "textbook" test

Concepts (go to frameworks and standards)

- Characteristics and life cycles
  - Three parts to their bodies
- Most insects have one pair of wings.
- They have six legs, and they have antennae.
- They are hatched from eggs; babies don't look like their parents.
- Most insects have four stages: Egg, larvae, pupa, and adult.
- Various cultures view insects differently.

Vocabulary (go to textbooks)

- Pair
- Pupa (cocoon)
- Antennae/feelers
- Egg
- Adult
- Metamorphoses
- Abdomen
- Exoskeleton
- Hatch
- Larvae

English language arts skills (go to ELA and ELD standards)

Choose as appropriate from overview.

Math, science, and social studies skills

Choose as appropriate from overview.

Resources and materials

- Fiction: Read aloud
  - *The Apple and the Moth*, Mari
  - *Very Hungry Caterpillar*, Carle
  - *The Little Blue Bug and the Bullies*, Poulet
  - *The Zoo in My Garden*, Nakatani
  - *If I Were a Cricket*, Mizumura
  - *Cricket in a Thicket*, poems
- Nonfiction
  - *Honeybee and the Robber*, Carle
  - *Preying Mantis: The Garden Dinosaur*
  - *Five Nests*, Arnold
  - *What's Hatching Out of That Egg?* Lauber
  - *Where Does the Butterfly Go When It Rains?* Garelick
  - *Chickens Aren't the Only Ones*
  - *Insects Do the Strangest Things*
  - *National Geographic*
  - *Zoobooks:* "Insects"
  - *Ranger Rick*: "Nature Scope"

GLAD Unit Planning Pages
Life in a Pond: Insects

Focusing and motivation

- Start silkworms
- Inquiry chart: What do we know . . . etc.
  - Read daily and process
- Ant farms

- Real honeycombs
- Entomologist awards

Input

- Pictorial input chart: Parts of insects, dragonfly for the pond; characteristics, names of different ones; three kinds of insects
- Narrative input: Life cycle of a dragonfly

Guided oral practice

- Form cooperative groups; pick an insect; each team draws, labels, and tells about their insect, adding information daily.
- Small group discussion of insect picture file cards: Categorize and classify; share results.
- Poetry: frames
- Personal interaction: Personal views about insects
- Observe and log or dictate observations of insects (live ones).
- Observe and log or dictate observations of an ant farm versus a spider—discuss.
- Team chanting for Big Books and poetry
- Brainstorming and team mind maps
- Farmer in the dell sentence patterning chart: insects

Reading and writing activities

- Total class
  - Expository: The life cycle of a dragonfly
  - Narrative: The story on an insect's life: Rufa the Wood Ant
- Flexible groupings: small groups
  - Cooperative
    * Flip chants and strip books
    * Mind mapping and story mapping
    * Practice group frame: Partner or group
    * Ear-to-ear reading with anticipation and prediction guide

 * Team Tasks
 * Peer conferences on readings and writings
 * Small group mini-lessons by teacher
 * Group reading practice and reinforcement of skills-leveled
 * ELD and SDAIE
- Individual
 * Personal exploration
 * Reading/writing choice time, as teacher takes dictation/records
 * Interactive journals
 * DEAR time
 * Individual conferences with teacher
 * Self-selected reading with response in log
 * Required writing to frames

Extended activities for integration

- Poetry frames: "I Know a Giant Dragonfly" or "Flies Here, Flies There"
- Art: Tissue paper butterflies, outlined in black construction paper; hide in bags (for cocoons)
- Work spaces with insects: How many eggs does your insect lay?
- Collecting folders of insects
- Collage of insects
- Taste honey: describe orally

Closure and evaluation

- Pancakes with honey
- Process all charts and learning.
- Make dragonfly Big Book with contact paper and iridescent cellophane paper for wings.
- Portfolio assessment conferences
- Share personal/team explorations.
- Ongoing assessment in logs

- Essay: Practice and use two reasons why insects help us and two reasons why they don't.

GLAD Idea Page
Life in a Pond: Amphibians

Unit theme

Amphibians are important as a test of the health of an ecosystem. They are unusual animals, and not reptiles.

Focusing and motivation

- Live tadpoles
- Inquiry charts: What do you know about amphibians?
- Interest Pieces: Brought in by teacher and students
- National Geographic: "The Colored Tree Frog"

Closure and evaluation

- Raffle off tadpoles (to consenting families)
- Process all charts and learnings
- Team Big Book
- Sketch and write: What you know about amphibians

Concepts (go to frameworks and standards)

- Life cycle: Eggs, young don't look like parents
- Characteristics: Wet skin, sheds skin, breathes under water and air through skin, webbed feet, cold-blooded
- Food chain and health of ecosystems
- Frogs versus Toads

Vocabulary (go to textbooks)

- Webbed
- Cold-blooded
- Gills/lungs
- Sheds
- Jelly-like
- Sucker
- Absorbed
- Other vocabulary from text and basals

English language arts skills (go to ELA and ELD standards)

Choose as appropriate from standards.

Math, science and history/social science

Choose as appropriate from standards.

Resources and materials

- Fiction
  - *Frog Went a Courtin'*, Langstaff
  - *Frog and Toad* series, Lobel
  - *The Frog Prince*, Anderson
  - *Olly's Pollywogs*
  - *A Frog in the Well*
  - *A Child's Book of Poems*
  - *Tim Tadpole and the Great Bullfrog*, Flack
  - *The Old Bullfrog*, Frescht
  - *The Toad Hunt*, Chaney
  - *Frog Goes to Dinner*, Mayer
- Nonfiction
  - *All Kinds of Babies*, Selsam
  - *National Geographic, Life in a Pond, The Green Tree Frog*

- *Ranger Rick*
- *Zoobooks*
- Teacher Rescources
  - *NatureScope, Ranger Rick, The Rainforest*
  - District texts
- Films and laser discs
  - *Amphibians: What, Where, and When*
  - *Gilly the Salamander*
  - *Windows on Science*

GLAD Unit Planning Pages
Life in a Pond: Amphibians

Focusing and motivation

- Observation charts: Kinds of amphibians
- Inquiry charts: Read and processed daily
- Chant: Down by the River Bank

Input

- Experiment: Add live tadpoles/eggs to water in aquarium/terrarium. Observe and record daily.
- Pictorial input chart: Parts, life cycle, and characteristics. Add to Living Wall.
- Narrative input of tadpole story. Kids retell and manipulate picture cards.

Guided oral practice

- T-graph for cooperation, coooperative groups
- Picture file activities: Comparing and contrasting
- Farmer in the Dell: Amphibians
  - Flip chant
  - Word cards taken to reading

- Expert groups: Kinds of amphibians
- Poetry and chanting
- Oral Book Sharing
- Personal interaction: Have you ever seen an amphibian? Felt one?
- Team tasks: Retelling of narrative, team picture, team mind map, team farmer in the dell, team flip chants, team strip books

Reading and writing

- Total class
  - Group frame, expository: Compare and contrast reptiles and amphibians.
  - Poetry frame
  - Story map
- Small group practice
  - Team tasks: Anything modeled by teacher
  - Choral and ear-to-ear reading
  - Team writing workshops
  - Author's chair
  - Guided Reading: Leveled
  - Expert group reading: Heterogeneous
  - ELD leveled groupings
- Individual
  - Personal exploration
  - Dictated or written required writings
  - Learning logs
  - Interactive journals and writing
  - DEAR time
  - Personal conferences with teacher

Extended activities for integration

- Songs: Froggy Went a Courtin'
- Team frog play or reader's theater
- Build terrarium and aquarium
- Directed art lessons for Big Books

Closure and evaluation

- Raffle off frogs or tadpoles
- Portfolio assessment conferences
- Process all charts and learnings
- Big Books to rubric

GLAD Idea Page
Life in a Pond: Plants

Unit theme

Plants are alive, as we are. We need plants to survive. Plants supply us with oxygen. Many plants on earth are endangered.

Focusing and motivation

- Relate to the water lily in the pond.
- View real plants with roots and seedlings.
- Inquiry charts
- Visualization: A plant grows.

Concepts

- Parts of a plant
- Needs of plants
- What humans can do to help with endangerment
- Photosynthesis

Vocabulary

- Root
- Stem
- Flower
- Pollen

- Blossom runner
- Fertilize
- Pistil
- Sepal
- Stamen
- Pollinate
- Tendril
- Other vocabulary from district texts

English language arts skills

Choose as appropriate from standards.

Math, science, and history/social science skills

Choose as appropriate from standards.

Resources and materials

- Fiction
  - *Seed, Seed, What Do You See?* (adaptation from Brown Bear)
  - *The Reason for a Flower*
  - *The Carrot Seed*
  - *Jack and the Beanstalk*
  - *Pussy Willow*
  - *The Giving Tree*
- Nonfiction
  - SCIS books and kits
  - AIMS project activities
  - *Ranger Rick*
  - *My Big Backyard*
  - *National Geographic World*
- Teacher resources
  - *Simple Science Experiments*
  - Macro Press

- *Ranger Rick:* "NatureScope Trees"
- Instructor study posters
- World Wildlife Foundation and the Sierra Club
- District texts
- Media
  - *Growing* (film)
  - *Secrets of the Plant World* (film)
  - *Wonders of Growing Plants*
  - Laser discs: *Windows on Science*
  - Internet: *LA Times* web site

GLAD Unit Planning Pages
Life in a Pond: Plants

Focusing and motivation

- Inquiry charts: Variation with groups, teams add two columns: Where can we find the answer? And five challenge questions for another team
- Collecting walk
- Collect and examine real plants, with roots and seeds.
- Movie: Walt Disney—*Secret Life of Plants*
- *The Important Book of Plants*

Input

- Pictorial input: The parts and life of a seed: Add to Living Wall.
- Experiments: (AIMS and Macro Press)
  - Celery in red food coloring
  - Plant four beans: One with soil, food, water, and light; one with soil, water, and no light; one with soil, light, and no water; one with light, water, and no soil. Discuss, predict, and chart growth.
  - Make soil: *Simple Science Experiments*

- Narrative input: Life of a plant, focusing on influence of weather and seasons (adaptation on *Carrot Seed*)
- Graphic organizer on types of plants

Guided oral practice

- T-graph on caring, cooperative groups
- Picture file activities: Categorizing, sequencing life cycle
- Sorting of real plants, seeds, leaves
- Chanting and poetry
- Process grid
- Expert groups
- Oral book sharing
- Oral story telling

Reading and writing

- Total class
  - Expository frame: Sequencing or cause and effect
  - Poetry frame
  - Narrative frame from story map
  - Modeled writing with verbalization
- Small group practice
  - Team tasks: Anything the teacher has modeled
  - Ear-to-ear and choral reading
  - Expert group reading (heterogeneous)
  - Big Books
  - SQ3R with partners
  - Peer conferencing and editing
  - Guided reading (leveled)
  - Reading partners with narrative
- Individual
  - Focused reading (reading/writing the walls)
  - Personal exploration
  - Required writings

- DEAR time
- Learning logs
- Interactive journals
- Personal conferences with teacher

Extended activities for integration

- Visualization: A walk around the pond
- Role play: Life cycle of a plant
- Grow real plants: All kinds
- Songs
- Movement
- Readers' theater
- Art: Solar printing, apple doll with seed face, fruit and vegetable printing

Closure and evaluation

- Plant party: Everybody brings a vegetable for soup.
- Game—Pin the Flower on the Plant
- Process all charts and learnings.
- Share personal and team explorations/Big Books.
- Portfolio assessment conferences
- Teach, model, practice multiple-choice exam.

GLAD Unit Planning Pages
Life in a Pond: Interdependence
of Life—Pulling It Together

Focusing and motivation

- Predicting charts: What would happen if there were no . . .?
- Film: Ecology—Living Things Depend on Each Other

Input

- Pictorial chart illustrating food chain: Ecosystem of a pond. Add to Living Wall.
- Living Wall: Life in a Pond. Students' art and print

Guided oral practice

- Teams draw and share a pond food chain.
- Roundtable list/group/label
- "Is this a Pond Ecosystem?" chant
- Farmer in the Dell: Endangered animals and review all Farmer in the Dells from unit.
- Process grid on parts of a pond ecosystem.
- Teams finish and present all team tasks.

Reading and writing

- Total class
  - Using process grid, cause and effects of endangerment
  - Teacher reviews all poetry frames presented in the unit.
  - Teacher reviews all narrative frames presented.
- Small group practice
  - T-graph on respect, cooperative
  - Team tasks, finish team paragraphs
  - Write a final team exploration of ecosystems.
  - Teams write "Where's My Answer" questions for final exam.

Closure and evaluation

- Personal exploration: To class/teacher developed rubric
- Huge Pond Party: Invite other classes, parents to view Living Wall, team tasks, and personal explorations.
- Process all charts and learnings.
- Assessment of unit folder on Life in a Pond

- Team presentations
- Where's My Answer review and final exam
- "Sketch and write everything you knew and I forgot to ask"
- Collect and assess unit folders on Life in a Pond.

5

Strategies

The creation of Living Walls and a Living Wall in the classrooms

What it is

In a language-functional environment, every chart or poem presented in the class is left on the walls to be read, processed, and added to on a daily basis. The walls become "alive" because they grow with the unit and the students. They are read daily by walking the walls or focused reading. They continue to be processed almost daily, highlighted, and discussed. They are added to so all students feel ownership with the walls and the poetry. Every unit is started with blank walls and the walls grow with narrative, pictorial, and graphic organizer input charts. As the unit progresses, the walls get filled with the language of the students as they acquire the content of the current unit. From this living environment comes a living wall. Usually stemming from a narrative or pictorial input chart, a living wall is a blend of pictorial, artistic, and linguistic input from teacher and students reinforcing a theme. The pictorial or narrative, student art, and student language come together to represent a theme in the content, making a Living Wall.

Personal interaction

> *I know sad. I sad on boat. My grandfather fall and get eated by sharks.*
>
> — 2nd grade student

Revelations like this and others that students have shared, such as having eggs and tomatoes thrown at them on the way to school; having adults yell "Go home, Gook"; and feeling the pressure of being pulled between two cultures, one of which shows no signs of completely accepting them, made us aware of the fact that our students were coming to school with personal experiences of an overwhelming nature. Because they were being given no time to share their frustrations or anger, it often affected their academic learning. The work of Bruce Baron, Irvine, CA, made us realize the need for setting up a structured opportunity in the classroom where feelings could be shared across cultures.

The other realization was that "Fun, Food, and Fiesta" is not enough to reduce prejudice (who ever stopped being prejudiced from eating egg roles or enchiladas?). People stop being prejudiced by working together in an environment structured to promote respect. Thus it was up to us to develop a classroom environment that taught and encouraged habits of positive interdependence. The personal interaction was a natural outgrowth.

What it is

Personal interaction refers to a specific time, directed by the teacher, to discuss issues or personal opinions on subjects, in partners and small groups. This is not the time for twenty to thirty-five students to share total class time. This is a strategy designed for student-to-student bonding, respect, and understanding. It is a variation on the 10/2 and used when issues come up at school, such as name calling on the blacktop, racism, prejudice, or any others that need discussion. Deal with the topics as they arise. Merely sending the offending student to the principal does not deal with the issue where it should be dealt with—with the students in your class. You may also use personal interaction time to discuss issues in literature, history, or science, when personal opinion is involved (not so factual).

How to do it

The teacher sets standards and expectations for these sessions. Important behaviors include active listening, patience, no interruptions, and appropriate responses. Chip talking can be used as a training device, if the students need it. Each student has a chip. One student puts his chip in the center. He talks until he is finished. No one can interrupt him until he says he is finished. The next student puts her chip in, and again no one can talk until she is finished. The first student may not talk again until all others have done so.

The amount of time for talking can be set by the teacher in advance or informally monitored while walking around the room. There may or may not be a quick total class sharing of what "my partner said," not what "I said."

Inquiry charts

These charts originated with inquiry science many years ago. Their appeal is such that they are used extensively beyond science, and triggered many variations.

What they are

Inquiry charts are vehicles for accessing and focusing background information, setting students purpose for learning, preassessing concepts, vocabulary, and grammar, processing the information learned on an almost daily basis, and determining how information was learned. The answers and questions that children give under

Strategies

What do we know about fish?	What do we want to learn?
	Challenge questions (for another team to answer) 1. 2. 3. 4. 5.

each heading have proven to be invaluable for ongoing diagnosis. These charts are also useful for modeled writing, modeling of the hypothesis model of science: predicting, studying, confirming, or refuting it, and rewriting it. We put our inquiry charts on butcher paper for ease of processing.

One column says "What do you know about . . .?" and the second says, "What would you like to learn?" Or "What were you wondering?" Or "What questions do you have?" Sometimes our third column has "Where do you think you might find the answer?" The KWL variation adds "What have we learned?" However, if you process these charts almost daily, the students will have a living idea of "what they have learned."

How we use them

The teacher records the students' answers the first day and adds new knowledge and questions every other day or so. These charts remain up during the entire unit for the teacher to process with the students. Questions the teacher will ask during the processing might include "How do we know that?" "Where did you find that answer?" "Did we find this to be a true statement? If not, can we change it to make it true?" "Is this the best way to say this? Can we say this differently to make it clearer (grammar)?" The hardest thing for teachers is to resist correcting students' original predictions at the time they are made. If you do, you defeat the purpose of this strategy, which is to teach students to predict based on their background knowledge and then to do some research and go back to self-correct. If you correct everything they say, why should they participate in this meaningless game?

Using color coding for each processing and, for younger grades, adding the student's name to the facts given can assist your emergent reader in rereading.

Variations

These include the following:

- Observation charts: Five to six pieces of tagboard are placed around the room with several pictures on each one. The pictures are tied to the content being studied. For example, planet observation charts would have nine pieces of tagboard, each with pictures of that planet. There is also a blank piece of unlined (usually large) paper where students write comments, questions, and predictions. This can be done in partners. From there on, these are processed like the inquiry charts. They are visual in nature and assist the second language learner.
- Predicting questions: The teacher puts a set of eight to ten predicting questions on students' desks as they come in. Students make predictions of answers and share with a partner. These are processed during the unit.
- Interest or challenge questions: The students come up with five to six questions at the beginning of the unit, and write these on a transparency. During the unit a team is chosen to challenge another team to answer the questions. This is like a family feud game. If they can, they get a point. If they can't, the challenging team gets the point. If the challenging team can't answer it, no one gets the point.

10/2 Lecture

What it is

This is a method of lecture, backed by brain-based research and presented by Art Costa (Training, FVSD). It is reinforced as well by Long, Swain, and Cummins, who state that it is important to allow at least two minutes of student processing with every ten minutes of teacher lecture. It is the two minutes that allows for comprehensible output, negotiating for meaning, and a risk-free environment to try new vocabulary and concepts with someone the student understands—another student. It allows metacognition. Also connected to brain research is the idea of chunking your information. People remember more information if it is chunked (as with your social security and phone numbers). So chunk your lecture, keep it to ten minutes at the most, and give a two-minute oral processing time.

We have adapted this also, and sometimes add a two-minute written processing after the oral. The other adaptation is to have students sit in primary language groups during lecture time, and have them process new concepts in their primary language first, then English.

Graphic organizers

What they are

The term graphic organizer, as we use it, refers to any nonlinear representation or organization of information. Brain research states that information is made retrievable over a longer period of time if it is taught in a pattern. This can also make information more comprehensible to your second language learner. In our model, for all forms of graphic organizers from pictorial input charts to time lines, we assist with the brain imprinting by having all sketches and vocabulary written in pencil first. Then, in front of the students, we go over the pencil sketch with marker, thus increasing brain imprinting. The more you vary the kinds of graphic organizers, the more models of organization students will have when developing their own. The following is only one of many kinds of graphic organizers.

Pictorial input chart

What it is

This is a pivotal strategy for making information comprehensible. The pictorial input chart is a key strategy in GLAD that can be used in all content areas. We originated this in our classroom because the

Graphic Organizer

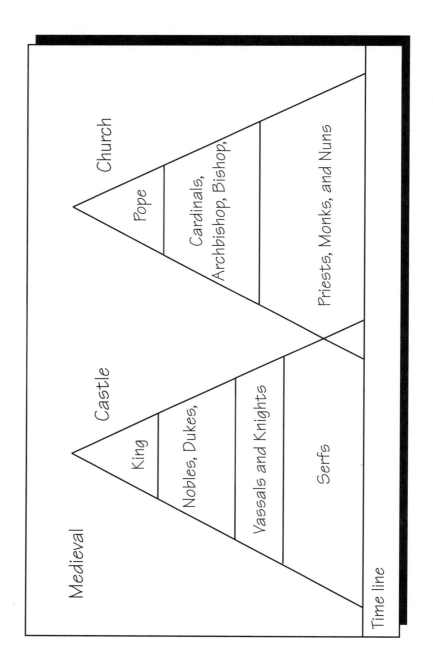

Medieval — Castle

King

Nobles, Dukes,

Vassals and Knights

Serfs

Church

Pope

Cardinals,
Archbishop, Bishop,

Priests, Monks, and Nuns

Time line

real things are not always available and this strategy helps take that place. When we wanted to be scientifically or historically correct, we would draw a facsimile in pencil of the pelican, layers of the sun, miner from the gold rush, and so on and take advantage of brain imprinting by going over the pencil in marker in front of the students. This gave the additional advantage of comprehensibility to the brain imprinting. Teachers across the nation have found this strategy to be a cornerstone for them, *once they learned the secret.*

How to use them

Using the Gold Rush miner as an example, put a picture of a miner under an opaque projector (or make a transparency for an overhead). Trace the figure, key concepts and vocabulary on a large piece of butcher paper, in pencil. Chunk your information to take advantage of brain research, put in the 10/2 lecture at each chunk, and you will have information easily understood, retained and retrieved. Even after the students catch on to the "secret," they are fascinated at what will develop.

We have used this strategy in grades K-8, varying the content. Pictorials of the wolf (K-1), to prehistoric people (6-7), the results are the same in over 100 school sites nationally: higher motivation, brain-compatible teaching, and more retention over time.

Variations

Comparative input charts follow the same process, but compare two figures. This is excellent as a character sketch comparing two literature figures such as Molly and Elizabeth in *Molly's Pilgrim* (B. Cohen). Comparing the characteristics, dress, and personalities of the characters helps provide background information and motivation to read the literature piece. When two figures are compared and contrasted, comprehension is increased and the oral pattern for that style of writing is modeled.

Narrative input charts take advantage of the strong oral language tradition of many students. High level, academic language and concepts are used but put into a story or narrative format. Many feel that if it is told in story or sequential format, the concepts must be watered down. The reverse is true. The story format allows for increased comprehension of academic concepts. While telling the story, pictures are used to increase comprehension.

The narrative input chart also provides a visual retelling (or preview) for your beginning ELD students. We have used this kind of chart in science, social studies, and literature. This input chart uses the narrative genre to teach many concepts or to introduce a literature piece, a visual preview. A teacher can also develop one for science using a narrative genre to convey scientific facts. Thus, a teacher might also sketch the background of a gold mining camp with an assay office, stamp mill and smelter, for which the students have little background information. The narrative or story might be the experience of one family in a mining town. Many important aspects of the gold rush can be presented, as well as comprehensibly delivered new vocabulary. Other examples are the retelling of a book, as with the *Seahorse*, by Robert Morris; the introduction to characters, setting, and plot in a literature piece; or to provide students with the oral patterning of a new genre (autobiographical incident). The teacher can also embed new concepts or vocabulary in narrative form. The narrative is told using grade-level concepts and vocabulary, with lots of patterning.

How to use it

In developing a narrative input within your content area, think of the new concepts or vocabulary to be embedded. If it seems to some like a large flannel board, it is. However, content-level concepts and vocabulary make it acceptable and useful for all grade levels. We have used it K–8.

After you have decided which ideas and vocabulary are to be taught, sketch an appropriate background. This can be as simple as a chalk sketch or as complicated as a mining town (which was traced on an opaque projector). Then develop the figures you will use to tell the story. These can be as simple as coloring books or copies (with permission) from a book, or drawn by the teacher or a student. As the story is told, the figures are put on the background. If you write the words on the back of each picture, you won't have to hold notes or worry about forgetting. In true narrative fashion, tell the story all the way through first, then ask for responses, questions and discussions with a 10/2 or personal interaction. An example of a narrative input is given in the sample unit section.

During reading/writing workshop, you will find students retelling the story to each other, changing names, characters, ending, and so on. In short, everything we try to get them to do after reading a story. Here they have the opportunity to do it orally first. The emphasis on patterning that remains around the room provides yet another example for students of the narrative format and the development of fictional characters. For the older students, it is a powerful way to model a new reading or writing genre.

Farmer in the Dell sentence patterning chart

What it is

This is a sentence patterning chart written on a large piece of butcher paper that assists students not only with vocabulary but also with parts of sentence and sentence structure. It is an adaptation on a chart first used by the McCrackens. It is an invaluable strategy that can be taken to reading, writing, and developing poetry. It provides a low anxiety environment in which to practice new vocabulary and unfamiliar sentence patterns.

How to use it

Draw four or five columns on a large piece of butcher paper, depending on grade levels. Grades K–3 would include adjectives, nouns, verbs, and prepositional phrases. Grades 4–8 might include adjectives, nouns, verbs, adverbs, and prepositional phrases. Each

139

Adjective	Noun	Verb	Adverb	Prepositional Phrase
sad tired lonely hard-working	miners	dig work shovel	quickly happily sadly	under the mountain in the rivers around mining camps

category is written in its own color. Label the columns using the correct academic term and a paraphrase. However, for success in teaching the strategy, give lots of prompts, especially with adverbs as these are difficult for most teachers. This is not a test. One doesn't expect a beginning ELD student to have memorized the definition; this is a teaching and practicing strategy. An example of a prompt for adjectives might be "Adjective, describing words. For example, look at those _____ they are so _____!" An example for prepositional phrases might be "Prepositional phrases, they tell us where the miners were digging, under . . . what, around . . . what, over . . . what."

The students brainstorm as many adjectives, prepositional phrases, and verbs as possible. Our suggestion is to use only one noun, and make that a plural. A plural noun means fewer problems with verb/subject agreement and no necessity for use of articles. When you are ready to teach single noun/verb agreement, model that for students before practicing. Then the teacher and students chant together, to the tune of Farmer in the Dell. Finally, students can volunteer to use the pointer and lead the class in chanting. The oral and reading practice is done over a number of days.

This can be taken to reading and writing by copying the words on word cards, using the same color as the chart. Groups are instructed to put together the most interesting sentences, using all the cards given (K–2, color coding is a must). Using numbered heads together, one student must read the sentence. The groups must help all to read to succeed. In older grades, mix the cards and throw several on the table. Tell them for the group to succeed, they must create a sentence with two adjectives, one noun, one verb, one adverb, and one prepositional phrase. If they do not have the necessary parts of speech, they must "go trading." The onus is put on the students to figure out what they have and what they need. This strategy works only after oral chanting of chart (hint for teachers of older students: I don't tell them that this is the Farmer in the Dell, only that it is a brain-imprinting chart for writing and sentence patterning).

Variations

We have adapted the Farmer in the Dell sentence patterning chart in many ways. To practice comparative and superlative adjectives, add a strip of paper that covers the adjective column, and brainstorm those. Replace present tense verbs with participles or past tense verbs, to meet specific ELA standards or SAT 9 practice. In one case, a fifth grade teacher asked if this could be used for teaching transitive and intransitive verbs (it worked!).

We suggest putting the chart where your word walls are. That way the students have one area in the room where they can look for their "doozers" or spelling challenges and their sentence "bank," to help with creating and expanding sentences. As with any such strategy, it is only as successful as the involvement of the students. Involve the students with the wall on a daily basis.

Process grids

What they are

Process grids are a variation on Sharon Bassano's wall grid. Hers was an excellent, mostly oral language grid. We have adapted it to all content areas. As its name implies, it is a grid with categories across the top and down the side (see graphic).

141

REPTILES

	Habitat	Food	Enemies	Life Cycle
Snakes				
Lizard				
Turtle				
Crocodile				

COMPARATIVE FAIRY TALES

	Characters	Setting	Plot	Solutions	Magic	Good/Evil
Cinderella						
Yen Chen						

How we use it

Students acquire information in a number of ways for the grid (background information, expert groups, or teacher input). They then dictate to the teacher with numbered heads together to increase habits of positive interdependence, using classifying and categorizing skills.

Process grids can be used to access prior knowledge, for authentic assessment and teaching the required writing domain. Higher level thinking skills are encouraged with questioning, predicting, generalizing, categorizing, and evaluating within the content areas. The teacher develops the category titles depending on the writing style she wishes to teach. Set your categories for compare and contrast, sequencing, or cause and effect, to name a few. The reason for this is that the process grid is most effective at teaching students how to write an expository paragraph.

Process grids can be later reproduced for use in teams and individually, with some intersections missing. Teams or partners question each other until the entire grid is completed.

The key to success here is to train students how to use this grid. It is sophisticated, and sometimes we expect students to know how to classify and categorize. Using numbered heads and structuring for success as you train the students how to do this will result in amazingly high-level thinking and production on the part of your students. Train them slowly. As teachers, we are too fast at jumping to the test, without scaffolding new strategies and concepts for success.

Kid grid

What it is

A kid grid is an excellent tool to use at the beginning of the year to encourage new friendships. If it is done right before a recess, students will know what other students' favorite activities are, so they can play together.

Good Friends' Kid Grid

Picture	Name	Favorite		
		Recess activity	Animal	Food
	Jenny			

How to use it

1. Form groups at a table with one adult to facilitate and write dictation. The children fill in a grid strip, and a bell rings every five minutes to change the category on the strip.
2. With the total group on the carpet, choose two or three kids' strips for modeling. Place on a bulletin board.
3. Read, ask questions, and get answers from students using the strips from the kid grid.

4. Next day, add more strips and continue processing.
5. Develop wall graph from information.
6. Sing "It's a Small World" together.

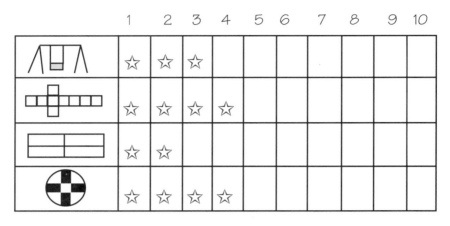

Picture file cards

What they are

Picture file cards are one of the most valuable tools an ELD teacher, or any teacher, can use. You must be prepared to think beyond the usual "What is this?" or "Point to the . . ." The worst thing that happened to picture file cards was ESL methodology. It usually directed teachers to very low-level activities for picture cards. Choose cards that are thought or emotion provoking for you. If they interest you, they will interest the students. If they interest the students, they will want to discuss them. If they are cut out of many sources (*National Geographic* is our favorite), then this will happen naturally. We have a general set to stimulate writing or for our library. The specific-to-unit-pictures we keep in a unit box, only brought out during that unit, so they remain of high interest.

144

How we use them (suggested activities)

There are numerous activities ranging from total class to individual, from oral language practice to writing, from directed teaching to follow-up and independent use. Here are a few suggestions:

- Direct teaching—Use them to make your teaching more comprehensible.
- Predicting—What is going to be taught or what is happening in the picture?
- Language building and language practice—Use new concepts and vocabulary that are stimulated by the pictures.
- Writing—Round table to teach the writing process or pictures to stimulate story writing.
- List, group, label—A GATE strategy, usually done in writing, develops higher level thinking on the part of your ELL. Students categorize their pictures, give each category a label, or title, and justify this to the class.
- Observation charts
- Developing questions
- Describing—Which picture am I describing?
- Assessment—Questions based on what has been taught, that the students can observe.

Hint: To develop these, pass out *National Geographic* and other magazines at the beginning of a unit. Instruct students that they must find as many pictures as they can about a particular topic. If they find one, they must show it to their group. If the group agrees that it fits the category, they may cut it out and paste it on a sheet of construction paper (remember to model what size you want). You will have over 100 picture file cards in forty minutes, and look at the higher level thinking that the students have done, classifying, categorizing, evaluating, and justifying.

Variation
Word bank cards
What they are

Word bank cards are like a small variation of picture file cards. They are especially useful with younger students (K–2) who love the tiny pictures. This idea came from "Skip" Herbert. Students may cut out pictures that are small for their own word bank. They must be able to say at least one thing about it. The teacher or student writes that word or phrase. The student keeps these words or phrases on a ring. As the student's language increases, more written words can be added. As with the picture file cards, many oral language activities can be done with these.

Cooperative learning
What it is

Cooperative learning is an extremely valuable tool in language acquisition. It is a vehicle through which cross-cultural interaction and oral language can be promoted. It allows a time and space for students to practice new concepts and vocabulary in a low anxiety environment, if we, as teachers, take the time to structure it for success. Cooperative learning also provides a vehicle for scaffolding, negotiating for meaning, comprehensible output, and guided oral practice. All of these terms are crucial for truly internalizing information and concepts. Cooperative learning also provides a much needed scaffolding if the groups are truly heterogeneous. To ensure use of appropriate social skills and cross-cultural respect, the use of the T-graph for social skills is strongly recommended. There are many models of cooperative learning: Kagen, Dishon, Johnson and Johnson, and they can all provide you with an in-depth study. We can only present a few examples here.

Roundtable: One piece of paper and one pencil, all must write, no one can write until the person before you writes. All can help with spelling and ideas.

Expert groups: This activity uses specially designed curriculum materials so that there is an extreme interdependence. Each member of the team has information crucial for the rest of the team to pass a test, fill a process grid, or do a written assignment. Numbering off the students in the group assures that the "expert" must pass on that information. You roll a dice, and the student whose number comes up must answer (and it may not be the expert). Allow them time to get back "heads together" to come up with the answer. This is only successful if the teacher takes the time to structure it so all can have success, including your English language learner.

Group frames and cooperative strip paragraphs

What they are

Following the whole to part model, the group frame allows the teacher to teach and model the conventions of writing. The teacher leads with a topic sentence for the required writing style: an expository piece, a lead-in for a narrative, or framing for poetry. Whatever genre the teacher wishes to model is the basis for this frame. The teacher provides the topic sentence and thus sets the stage for a comparing and contrasting paragraph, a sequential, or a cause and effect paragraph. The planning by the students can occur through mind-mapping, sketching, process grid, listing, or just talking. Gathering ideas from other writers in the room is encouraged here. We usually utilize the group frame for younger writers or emergent writers with dictation.

The cooperative strip paragraph is an adaptation of Nancy Whistler's model and the group frame. The teacher also provides the topic sentence, and the students provide the supporting details from the process grid. This time, they write their own sentences, only after orally agreeing on it. Each team can develop a paragraph—sometimes each group comes up with one supporting sentence for a topic sentence provided by the teacher. Alternately, they can come up with the topic sentence and supporting details. Each team can come up with one stanza or each team can come up

147

with one phrase of a stanza they have developed from a preexisting poetry frame or one they have developed. This strategy allows for negotiating for meaning and an anxiety-free environment for practice in developing any kind of text. It also allows for authentic revising and editing because the students will have written the text. This strategy models the writing process, teaches writing skills, and metacognition or quality of writing. It is also typed up and used for emergent reading.

How we use it

From this point on, the process is the same with dictation or cooperative strip paragraphs. The students read the piece together and highlight the things that are high level, that they like, or that they think make the writing interesting or compelling. They can also share their response in general terms to the writing (the responding part of the writing process).

The students then read to see if it makes sense or if there are any suggestions. This is revising—the most often ignored part of writing and the most crucial to develop quality writers. As Krashen stated (Remarks: CABE, 1992), "Merely writing does not make one a better writer, reading and thinking about your writing (metacognition) makes one a better writer." In the beginning, the teacher suggests that perhaps the order could be changed to make better sense, some words or sentences added or combined, perhaps some taken out. All of these suggestions can be followed through with a pair of scissors, extra sentence strips and markers. The teacher models with suggestions he/she might make and discusses the reasoning with the students. The emphasis is on metacognition, the ease of revising, and how the writing often improves with suggestions from others. Though at the beginning of the process the teacher does the majority of the modeling and discussion of why changes are made, as the students become more comfortable with the process, they will have more input on the revisions.

The last step is to teach and model the editing process. Taking one skill at a time (e.g., spelling or punctuation), the class reads and makes suggestions. The key here is to not expect your students to edit for any skill that they have not been taught. In other words, your first grader may not be able to check for certain spellings or grammatical structures. This sounds elementary, but how often do we red line a first-grade student's paper for failing to do correctly something that they have not been taught.

Students will utilize this modeling of responding, revising and editing with their editing checklist during the in writer's workshop. The value of modeling the cooperative strip paragraph first is that no one person has possession of this poem or paragraph; thus, there is less resistance to changing it. The other advantage of this strategy is that it becomes authentic daily oral language practice.

We then recopy the group frame or cooperative strip paragraph, whether dictation or cooperative strip, after it has been responded to, revised, and edited. The teacher is the publisher and the final editor. Once copied on the computer, each student gets a copy and this becomes important reading practice for the student, with silent, partner, and directed reading. In flexible reading groups or with individuals, the teacher can teach and reinforce appropriate reading skills in context and help the students develop their own personal spelling list, directly tied to their writing. With emergent readers, at any grade level, if the group frame is done at leveled groups, you will truly have copies of leveled reading, regardless of grade level. For struggling older readers, this student-generated text is crucial to begin content-based reading. Then take the students through the last five steps of the language to literacy cycle.

The language to literacy cycle: Teacher copies student-dictated paragraph or cooperative strip paragraph, matching colors used by students on original, incorporating any agreed-upon editing, on sentence strip with students watching, and verbalizing various mechanics (capitals, period, and so on). Students reread mix up sentence strips. Following that they put the paragraph back in order with the original chart always showing. They reread.

- Teacher and students reread paragraph. Teacher cuts sentences into phrases (students count how many words are in a phrase), mixes them up, students put the paragraph back in correct order and *proves* it by reading the sentences.

Asking the students, "Are you right?" or "Are you correct?" and "Can you prove it to me?" becomes a metacognitive aspect of the reading cycle. Too often, we make students too teacher-dependent when we affirm if they are right or wrong. Here, they can prove it by reading it back aloud and matching with the original chart when necessary. This builds feelings of confidence and self-efficacy. However, the first time you ask "Are you correct?" they will change their answer, because so often we only ask it when they are wrong. Instead, it should become a stock question whether the student is right or wrong. It encourages students to think about their answers and how they found them.

After manipulating the phrases several times, the teacher cuts phrases into word cards, mixes them up and students put them back in order and "proves it" by reading aloud. The original chart is still visible to students.

• Teacher and students reread chart. Students put word cards in order to form original paragraph or part of the paragraph. One of the many emergent reading activities we use is the modified cloze technique for words in context. Students close their eyes, the teacher removes one word, students open eyes and guess which word is missing. Students again prove it by reading the sentence aloud. Repeat this several times, allowing the students to take turns removing the word. Going from whole to part allows the students to develop the concepts of sentences and words. This also allows discussion of skills in context and words in context as well as developing vocabulary and spelling words. Many other reading activities can be done here. The clue game can follow: teacher gives a "clue," which can be an initial sound, letter, or antonym/synonym, then students give clues. Word cards used for this game can become flash cards for sight words also.

• Student and teacher review all that has been acquired and decide whether or not to add to the paragraph or poem or to illustrate. Students dictate or write, if capable, their own paragraph.

Thus, the group frame is a vehicle for teaching and modeling the process of writing in the various genres and is used as a reading tool, once developed.

The cooperative strip paragraphs are used to teach the writing process to the entire class and in teams. Everyone participates in highlighting the strengths, revising, and editing the copy. The teacher is the final editor and types it for reading.

Next, the same topic sentence is used, and teams develop a strip paragraph together. This is used for team read-arounds, revising and editing suggestions.

Finally, the students follow the process and write to the teacher's topic sentence individually. This follows the scaffolding model: a balance of total class, small group practice, and individual use. All these student-generated texts are used for teaching and practice of reading skills. This provides a much needed scaffolding for successful writing. It also provides close-to-grade-level reading for upper level students. Because you have built the academic language for at least one to two weeks, the language that they will produce is closer to grade level reading than they would ever get otherwise. What they can understand and say, they can write or dictate; what they can write or dictate, they can read. (Sound familiar?) A management tip is that the infamous *blue pocket chart* really is most efficient for teaching students how to revise, even at the upper grades.

Team tasks

What they are

We use these in place of centers. Anytime we are pulling a flexible group, we have the students working on team tasks. These ultimately become individual tasks. We try to make sure that many modalities are represented. Anything the teacher has modeled is appropriate for a team task, because these become the basis of individual use, thus providing practice or scaffolding for individual use.

Some examples: Team flip chants, team story map, team timeline, team Farmer in the Dell, team map, ear-to-ear reading, team cooperative strip paragraph, team process grid, team "research read," team SQ3R, team mind-map, team map, team sentences from Farmer in the Dell, discussing center, team action plans, team interviews. Team blends from words on walls, team-rhyming banks, team words from unifix cubes, team "reading game" (modified cloze) with cooperative strip paragraph.

Poetry frames

What it is

A poetry frame is a poem that lends itself to being adapted and expanded by students. These poems or chants can also be adapted for any unit. The new content vocabulary is exchanged for the old, and instantly, you have a low affective filter way to practice new vocabulary. After trying a few of these poems or chants with trepidation, you will become addicted to developing them (as do the students). Remember that they are used not just for fun, but rather for several important educational reasons: the importance of patterning that comes out of brain research; the chance to use new vocabulary from the negotiating for meaning research; and the low affective filter of trying new words with no one looking at you, from the language acquisition research. If it seems a bit uncomfortable in the beginning, remember, it's not about you. We as teachers need to stretch ourselves if it means assisting even a small group of our students.

How to use it

The following frames can be used with any unit. Listen to the syllables, know your content and vocabulary, remove the words here, and insert the new content vocabulary and concepts.

Winds here, winds there
Winds, winds everywhere.
Hurricane winds storming
Tornado winds circling
Breezy winds puffing
Blizzard winds driving

Scirroco winds from the desert
Mistral winds in the Mediterranean
Chinook winds through the Rockies
Kamizaki winds around Japan

Winds here, winds there
Winds, winds everywhere
WINDS! WINDS! WINDS!

This poem first came to us from the McCrackens (Training 1986) with Christmas here, Christmas there. We have adapted it K–8. Middle school vocabulary is inserted: Cro-Magnon here, Cro-Magnon there, Energy here, Energy there. Because of its direct link to the sentence patterning chart (Farmer in the Dell), it is easy to develop a frame for your English language learners to use to begin developing their own chants. Replace lines three through ten with words generated by the Farmer in the Dell. Model first, total class, then have teams develop one.

The Rap

I'm a botanist and here to say,
I study all living things and that's OK.
Sometimes I write a paper, sometimes I read a book,
But, usually, I go and take a look.

Plants, animals, monerans, too
Doing the classification bugaloo!

There are 5 Kingdoms, so I'm told,
All living things go into, young or old.
Most plants and animals, we all know,
But, monerans and fungi, too strange, no?

> Plants, animals, monerans too
> Doing the classification bugaloo!

Animal, Protist, Moneran too,
Plants, and Fungi, 5 Kingdoms for you.
Next time you study Living Things, it's true
You are doing the classification bugaloo.

> Plants, animals, monerans too
> Doing the classification bugaloo!

Taking advantage of the rap movement, the bugaloo has been a favorite of all grades. Older students have done the "Archeologist Bugaloo." First written by Andy Brechtel (I'm a Crustacean), it has since been used by five eighth-grade graduation speakers in San Jose instead of their graduation speeches. Yes, "big" kids love these!

Cinderella (to I'm a Nut)

Cinderella, good as gold,
Works all day, so I've been told.
Scrubs and scrubs but still stays clean.
She has two sisters ugly and mean,
They laugh at her and call her names,
When things go wrong, it's her they
> Blame.

> C-I-N-D-E-R-E-L-L-A!
> C-I-N-D-E-R-E-L-L-A!

Then there's the prince, not too smart
Without the shoes, can't tell them apart.

Handsome is as handsome does,
Sends someone else to look because,
He's the prince, stays at the castle,

Doesn't look, doesn't like the hassle.
C-I-N-D-E-R-E-L-L-A!
C-I-N-D-E-R-E-L-L-A!

This frame came to us from Fred Bitner, an eighth-grade teacher, who, with extreme trepidation, attempted this with his literature class for *Call of the Wild*. He said that it was the only chant he knew (from being a camp counselor). Fred put a summary of each chapter into a stanza, then he added clapping to the tune of "We Will Rock You." His class loved it, as have all the classes where it has been presented. Variations have included "I'm a fox, small and brown"; "I'm a tiger, striped and strong," and so on.

One of our favorite vocabulary practice chants came from Ella Jenkins, "Did You Feed My Cow?" We removed her words and inserted new vocabulary (with apologies to Ella). Variations have included "Is this an Ecosystem?" and "Are these the Clovis people?" The beat and rhythm will get even older students involved if the vocabulary is at grade level. Patterning works!

Yes, Ma'am

Is this energy?   Yes, ma'am
Is this energy?   Yes, ma'am
How do you know?   It's changing or moving.
How do you know?   It helps us work.
Give me some examples.   Mechanical and heat
Give me some examples.   Nuclear and chemical

Is this potential energy?   Yes, ma'am
Is this potential energy?   Yes, ma'am

How do you know?
How do you know?
Give me some examples.
Give me some examples.

It may move.
It has stored energy.
Wood and food
Rubber band and batteries

Is this kinetic energy?
Is this kinetic energy?
How do you know?
How do you know?
Give me some examples.
Give me some examples.

Yes, ma'am
Yes, ma'am
It's moving or changing.
Gravity pulls it down.
An arrow and fire
A rock falling down

And are you through?
Did you tell me true?
What did you chant?
What did you chant?

Yes, ma'am
Yes, ma'am
Energy!
Energy!

Marine Cadence

We just know what we've been told,
Meteorology's worth its weight in gold.
Studying weather here and there,
Forecasting weather everywhere.

> Sound off - Meteorology
> Sound off - Weather forecasting
> Sound off - One, two, three, four I'M COOL!

Tornadoes circle round and round,
Lift those houses off the ground.
On the land, tornadoes we fear.
They move our houses everywhere.

> Sound off - Tornadoes
> Sound off - Twisters
> Sound off - One, two, three, four DUCK LOW!

Hurricanes almost the same,
Circle - round with a different name.
The difference is quite plain to see,
Hurricanes start out in the deep blue sea.

> Sound off - Hurricanes
> Sound off - Cyclones
> Sound off - One, two, three, four RUN FAST!

This frame is another example of summer camp chants. Sterling came home humming this tune. Extract the current vocabulary and insert yours, and Voila!

A content-based frame, it has become the "Trust March," "We just know what we've been told, archeology's worth its weight in gold," and many others. A fifth-grade class turned this into their room chant: "We just know what we've been told, Room 22 is good as gold. We study here, we study there, Room 22 studies everywhere. Sound off—Awesome. Sound off—Studies Hard. Sound Off—1-2-3-4- That's Us."

The Important Thing

The important thing about wolves is they are endangered.
> They are strong and they are smart.
> They are playful with each other.
> They protect their puppies well,
> both the father and mother.

But, the important thing about the wolf is that it is endangered.

The important thing about wolves is they are endangered.
> They are *in* the family "Wild Dogs"
> with others of their kind.
> Coyote, fox, dingo, dhole
> are also there, you'll find.

But, the important thing about the wolf is that it is endangered.

157

The important thing about wolves is they are endangered.
>One is strongest, hunt or play
>he's dominant, they say.
>He leads the pack to hunt their prey
>cooperation is their way.

But, the important thing about the wolf is that it is endangered.

The important thing about wolves is they are endangered.
They're strong and smart but fairy tales all make them mean and angry
>Wolves never eat the people really
>not even when they're hungry

But, the important thing about the wolf is that it is endangered.

More in the nature of a free–form poem, this frame has become a staple for the teacher-made big books. It highlights critical attributes and can model key grammatical items (notice verb–subject agreement on top and bottom of the page). The top and bottom of the page, with this frame, usually contain the theme of the unit being taught. At middle school, it became, "The important thing about survival."

I Know

I know a Giant Panda
>An enormous Giant Panda
>An enormous Giant Panda,

With black eye patches,
>Black and white colored,
>Thick, rough fur,
>Strong, crunching molars
>And strong, black claws

I know a Giant Panda
>An enormous Giant Panda
>An enormous Giant Panda

Who sleeps with me.

This was the first totally original frame attempted by the author. It was very simplistic, for first grade. However, it has become: "I Know an ancient people," for sixth and seventh grades, and a very evocative poem "I Know an Immigrant Child."

I know a tiny sea horse,
teeny, tiny sea horse,
a teeny, tiny sea horse,
With a long, thin snout.

A prehensile tail,
small bony rings,
a fast dorsal fin,
And babies in his pouch.

I know a tiny sea horse,
a teeny, tiny sea horse,
a teeny, tiny sea horse,
With a long, thin snout.

I know an immigrant child,
a young immigrant child,
a young immigrant child,
who wants to be happy.

He dreams of having friends,
that won't make fun,
friends that he can trust,
Who won't carry a gun.

She dreams of having food,
a coat in the cold,
a dress to be admired,
A new doll to hold.

I know an immigrant child,
the same as you and me,
we all have similar needs,
Now don't you see?

We all were once immigrants
in a strange, new place,
looking for a better life
With hopes and dreams to face.

These are only a few of the frames that teachers can utilize to take advantage of patterning, a low affective filter, and negotiating for meaning. As the saying goes, "try it, you'll like it."

Listen and sketch

What it is

The teacher reads a short book in small chunks. After each chunk (about two to three paragraphs), the teacher instructs the students to "sketch the picture in their head." This encourages students to visualize, a skill that most struggling readers don't have. This is not a beginning ELD strategy. It is most effective when used in later stages of ELD. To use this strategy successfully, the students must be taught the difference between sketching and drawing. We tell them that sketching is for your brain and drawing is for art. Although highly simplistic, it seems to sum up the difference for younger students. We use "sketch and write" in logs, journals, and assessment tools, thus allowing more access to ELD and visual learners.

Personal exploration

What it is

This concept was adapted from Jerry Treadway. Its importance is reinforced by research on metacognition and multiple intelligences. It is the chance at the end of a unit for a student to choose the method he/she will use to demonstrate what has been learned and acquired. Students may choose to do this by means as varied as drawing, writing poetry or chants, building models, or using a hypercard presentation.

How to do it

Teachers and students develop the rubric together. A word of caution: If the rubric is set up ahead of time and well understood, there is no problem. Decide if you are developing the rubric on content or form. It is difficult for students who write a piece of personal poetry for their personal exploration to be assessed on form, unless that was understood at the onset and they knew they were writing to that form. For example, two raps on the American Revolution were assessed based on the content rubric; students had to demonstrate an understanding of the causes of the revolution and some of the individuals involved. Students were not graded on the quality of the rap or the rhyming. The students will amaze you with their creativity. Sharing these explorations is a wonderful way to spread ideas for other students to use next time and also to celebrate the end of a unit by sharing personal projects.

Sketch and write is also an excellent way to finish the unit. After having given the "real test," ask the students to sketch and write everything they knew that the teacher had forgotten to ask. Many of us have left tests feeling that we knew more than they asked. This is another way to include your ELD and divergent learner in the assessment process.

Writer's workshop

What it is

The majority of our students' most incredible poems and chants (as well as other personal writings) come from the workshop. We have adapted Lucy Calkins' model. However, we agree with Donald Graves recommendation when he said, "If anyone tells you that there is only one way to do it, walk out." Many teachers have their own variations. The key points that encourage writing are as follows:

1. All writing during this time is free choice. *We do not use prompts or trigger words.* We find that when your walls drip with language and modeled writing, prompts are unnecessary and limiting. Remember, you have the group frame or learning logs for students to respond to prompts.

2. The *short* mini-lesson of no more than five minutes provides ample modeling. Remember, the mini-lesson is not a time to

teach the nineteen things you think the students don't know about writing. Use your group frame to teach those skills. Keep to the five-minute rule. This part is important for modeling quality of writing. This can be done by reading published authors, kids' writings from other years, or your writing. The mini-lesson can also be for prompting, modeling of choice, kinds of writing, class discussion on the workshop itself and its process, or other short aspects of writing. You might remind the students on a revising or editing skill that you worked on with the group frame. You might notice that several students are having trouble ending their stories. You might model how several different authors ended their stories in different ways. There are many things to model here.

3. Ample time for the actual writing. It is important to note that we encourage sketching and mind-mapping at all ages. If sketching becomes a part of prewriting, both sides of the brain combine to produce language. We encourage students at all grades and English ability to sketch (not draw—drawing is for art, sketching is for the brain) not just as a prewriting step, but also as a way to remember information and add to the writing. Conferencing by the teacher occurs at this time. Conferencing is another opportunity for the teacher to foster that metacognitive aspect of writing. It is here that the teacher discusses the progress of a student's writing. The emphasis is on the nudging forward of a student's writing. Remember, as teachers, we can nudge, hint, and make suggestions until the students' writings match the ideas in our heads, and what will we have accomplished? We will have taught them to depend on us and our evaluations and suggestions. The underlying concept is that the students need to become more critical readers of their own work. That is why we work so hard at modeling the metacognitive aspect of writing. That is also why we encourage a peer editing or three-before-me editing (from the UCI Writing Project). Students utilize the modeling done during the group frame to make suggestions for each other's writing. Authors, of course, have the right to accept

or decline peer suggestions. Just as with revising, responding, and editing, conferencing can occur with one student or a few, if all involved are interested in discussing the same aspect of writing, such as the beginning or ending of a narrative.

4. Author's chair becomes a key item in the workshop, with the emphasis on the metacognitive aspect of the chair. We share unfinished work or work in progress in author's chair. As such, no one claps because the purpose is not show and tell, but rather helping each other become better writers. Also, the teacher has no part in the front of the room. He/she takes a seat with the audience. In order to respond or ask a question of the author, the teacher must also raise his/her hand and wait to be called upon. The sharing of work in progress encourages others to try types of writing they normally might not have tried. Some educators, Lucy Calkins included, express some difficulty in getting children to write poetry. We believe, as does Gabrielle Rico, that we have a more instinctive ability to write poetry than expository. Because it is modeled by the teacher, is present on the walls, used daily by the students, presented in Poetry Booklets and encouraged through the mini-lesson, our students find poetry a natural expression of themselves and the content.

How we do it

1. Don't try to do everything at once. Add conferencing and publishing after the students are in the routine of mini-lesson, planning/writing, and author's chair.

2. Keep your mini-lesson to five minutes. Do not try to teach the kids every writing skill in one session. Model and remind students of choices and/or skills previously taught.

3. Response guide for author's chair: "I like the part where . . .," "I think you might try . . .," "I'd like to know more about . . .," "I was confused where . . .," "If you add the descriptive words

_____, _____, or_____ I could visualize the scenes better." (The emphasis on *I* indicates that the suggestion is the listeners' issue and not the author's problem.) "Will you be adding more?" "What gave you the idea for this piece?" Remember, stress the metacognitive—the purpose is to make us better writers. Save clapping for your publishing parties. Remember, the author does not have to take any suggestions. The author just responds with "Thank you." When presented this way, students welcome suggestions in the author's chair. One first grader was experimenting with changing "I Know An Unusual House" to "I Know an Unusual Dog." He got stuck after the first verse, shared his start during author's chair, asked for suggestions and was bombarded with excited offers from numerous other authors. Of course, rather than listen to others in the author's chair, he immediately wanted to return to his desk and incorporate most of the suggestions.

4. Have a writing corner with paper (of all kinds), scissors, pencils, markers, staplers, sentence strips, strips of construction paper. Train your students to use it as needed, without having to ask you.

5. Conferencing is an important part of assessing your students' progress and providing meaningful nudges to your students in their early drafts. If students are choosing to tell their story in pictures, use the same kind of nudges that you would with writing. "Tell me what your story is about," "I think another picture here might help me see that more clearly," and so on.

6. In older grades, encourage students to keep a folder where they revisit previously written items to extend, shorten, change. Teach revising and editing with your group frames and cooperative strip paragraphs. Practice with three-before-me editing, during publishing time. Have a parent or older student help with publishing once or twice a week. Students get used to the flow. Students can also be encouraged to develop read-around groups when a number of them are ready at the same time.

7. Have reading and writing choices available: Pocket poetry (or ring poetry), narrative input charts, cooperative strip paragraphs, poetry around the room and in the poetry booklet, a research corner with all content-focused books and magazines such as *Zoo Books* or *National Geographic*, picture file cards, frames, and for younger writers, opportunities for literacy events around the room such as message pads by the telephone in the housekeeping corner, a grocery pad on the refrigerator, checkbooks (name and number blank, of course), cash register and order blanks for the store corner, subscription blanks and prescription blanks for zoo or doctor's corners. In other words, provide opportunities for authentic writing.

8. Enjoy and appreciate the wonderful authorship of your students. (It is the most important part of the process.) Share what you have written as well.

Truly, writer's workshop helps the students discover the voices within.

Big Books

"Patterning and predictable language is a key feature of many Big Books. Repeated readings make Big Books a rich resource of language activities such as tracking print, think along activities, cloze activities, and examining text features."

—Dorothy Strickland, 1990

What they are

Teacher-made Big Books fill a unique need in the classroom. They address specific content and linguistic needs of each individual classroom and curriculum without the enormous expense usually needed to acquire content area Big Books that even halfway meet a teacher's needs.

The research and writings in the fields of psycholinguistics, reading, and the brain all agree on the importance of that metacognitive aspect of accessing and building background information. Teachers can embed concepts and high level vocabulary specific to a unit with comprehensibility and patterning to assure that it is understood and retrievable over a long period of time.

Why should teachers make their own Big Book? There are many fiction Big Books available, and fiction does contain a magic that can enchant listeners and stretch their imaginations. The sound and rhythm of the language used in the narrative mode brings characters to life, enables children to visualize other settings and times, engages them in the lives of others, and touches familiar themes common to all people. "Quality fiction engages children in the meaning-making process that educators have come to recognize as the essence of literacy." (R. Doiron, *Reading Teacher*, 1994). There are, in fact, some wonderful, purchasable Big Books in the narrative mode. However, keeping in mind that we use Big Books to provide a comprehensible, motivating focus for the unit you are teaching, it is difficult to find Big Books that emphasize the content, narrative style, and vocabulary that you wish to present.

Also, people like Pappas (1991) have seriously challenged the notion that narrative should play such a dominant role in literacy programs. He warns that, with an almost exclusive emphasis on narrative, we could create a barrier to full access to literacy by providing children with little experience reading and writing nonstory texts.

Research on patterning reinforces this. From kindergarten, we provide students with the "once upon a time" story pattern. We seldom read aloud expository patterns. In third grade, when texts become expository in nature, the students without the pattern seem dyslexic. Leanna Traill adds to this by suggesting that we model our read aloud to the type of text that we are reading. For example, if it is a short dramatic piece, then read it that way the first time through. If it is a piece from a newspaper or encyclopedia, one doesn't read these cover to cover; pictures and heading add to our decision of what and how we will read. The works of Collier and Thomas (1995) and Chamot and O'Malley (1994) further reinforce the importance of content-based English as a means of acquiring a language.

Finally, there has been a shift in the role of the teacher from one who is "filling empty vessels" to the teacher as a facilitator, audience, model, and co-participant in learning. Providing models or demonstrations of literacy is a key part of this new paradigm. Cambourne speaks to this, as do many others. The key idea is that the text is placed in the center of development of literacy. There is a need for a strong concept of authorship to pull together skills and elements of literacy. Making your own Big Books is a marvelous way to demonstrate your authorship and model your development of a piece of literature or text.

How we develop and use them

Nonfiction

- Complete your research of the topic to be studied. Look for "big ideas," key concepts, key vocabulary, or phrases. Look for ones that stir your interest. (Hint: You will find these more often when reading books other than the standard teacher text, *National Geographic*, for example). Remember to retain the integrity of the selection of concepts and vocabulary in the creation of nonfiction books.
- Look for phrases that could become part of a pattern. Some of our successful patterns are:
  - "the important thing about the Sun is . . ."
  - "I'm concerned about the ocean . . ."
  - "I just thought you might like to know . . ."
  - "Who were you who trod so lightly on the earth?"
  - "America is a country of immigrants and refugees. Why did your family come to America?"
- Look for several key concepts to add with the pattern. These are often placed between the key concepts. Many times, it looks like this:

Key pattern phrase

First key concept
Second concept
Third concept
Closing pattern phrase

Remember, this is a tool to introduce a subject and hook/ motivate your students. Think major concepts/thoughts. You don't need to add all concepts to this book. As Mark Twain said, "Brevity is the soul of wit." We have had some very successful, longer teacher-made Big Books, but they are the exception, not the rule. (Acid test: Read it to your own children and young people from your neighborhood, at the appropriate age, before and after revisions.)

- Once you have your "big ideas," put it together in rough draft and think about what art form goes well with it. Art can consist of anything from a collage of pictures from magazines to a more advanced art form (great way to start a directed art lesson).

Fiction or poetry

This format mirrors the process for teacher-generated poetry and part of the nonfiction. Key concepts and key vocabulary are the starting place. In the area of fiction, other ideas should be considered. Perhaps this is a tool for the comprehensible presentation of the setting and character comparison of a new literature piece. The difference with fiction is that, although you are embedding concepts and vocabulary, you do not want to rewrite the original fiction piece. Do not give away the story. Rather take the major concepts (like survival in *Island of the Blue Dolphin* or the immigration experience in *Molly's Pilgrim* [B. Cohen, 1983]) and develop your Big Book around that.

Almost every Big Book takes on the feeling of poetry. Fred Bittner, one of the teachers we worked with, came up with a good example of that. He was introducing *Call of the Wild*, by Jack London, and his text used poetic devises to introduce each chapter of the novel. His eighth-grade students were clamoring to read the book when he was finished.

There are various opinions on whether to bind, hinge, or number pages or not. If the pages are not hitched or numbered, students can use them for retelling or sequencing. However, from the teacher's viewpoint, it can help to have them linked together, or numbered, for ease and speed.

Teacher-made Big Books are intended to *introduce* a subject, concepts, language patterns, and/or vocabulary. As such, it is used at the beginning of a unit, during *Focusing and motivation*, for accessing and focusing background information and motivating students. It can be, as well, an introduction to an art medium about which you intend to give a directed art lesson later in the unit.

1. The first reading should be done straight through. Try not to stop for definitions or explanations. The students need the feel of the language and the flow. Ask for responses/questions. This is a perfect time for a 10/2 or a personal interaction. Get students' immediate response. Then go back and go more slowly, discussing words in context. Leanna Traill (Training, 1994) helped us realize the value of reading text to students as we would read it. It is a major premise of shared reading. As suggested by Traill, don't destroy a short, dramatic piece by overanalysis (just look what happened to our attitudes towards poetry when teachers did that). There is also the cognitive aspect. We need to model how we, as literate adults, read. If it is a short piece, or book, we read it straight through. If it is longer, or certain kinds of expository (such as newspapers or encyclopedias) we don't always read from beginning to end. Instead, we focus on what we want to know and skip around as we read for information. The importance here is to maintain the integrity of the piece.

2. Upon second readings, or during the first, if you can do so without interfering with the integrity of the piece, the emphasis in discussion should be on meaning. An emphasis on story meaning leads to superior performance on an array of outcome elements, including recall of propositions, short answers to questions, recall of important elements, oral reading errors, story

interest, and lesson time. The difference is especially notable for children in low and average groups.

Writing process for developing fictional characters

What it is

The following is a process to actually teach students how to develop fictional characters when writing in that mode. It is a process that goes from teacher modeling to individual writing. This is a natural progression from a narrative input chart. During the narrative input chart, you have modeled the genre orally for the students. This part of the writing process is not a beginning of the unit strategy. Students must have some content information already or you need to develop expert groups for the information. Here you will model how to write it.

How to do it

First, set up interest corners around the room. For example, if you are studying Native Americans, you might have five pieces of butcher paper in different areas of the room. (Anasazi, Mound Builders, the Clovis People, pre-Clovis, and Western Coastal). Students read each and write their names on the pieces of paper with the heading of the people they would like to write about. They also write one reason why. Pictures on each paper can remind students about each group.

Second, students get together by groups of people with the same interest. They brainstorm facts they know about the period and the people. Individuals write these facts on their own graphic organizers. Basically, these can be separated into "Facts About the Period": Weather, Time, Culture, Development, People; and "Facts About the People": Clothing, Jobs, Food, Housing, and so on.

Next, using facts from the first two organizers for the setting and background, the students each do a quickwrite for their character.

Students return to their original group of four (not interest groups) and do quick read-arounds. The teacher makes these read-arounds move quickly. Students pick out one specific thing from each paper that they agree makes it authentic or vivid (or any other writing skill you are working on). The group reads that section to the class.

Third, students develop a graphic organization for their own character:

> Character: Name, Likes, Dislikes, Friends, Enemies, Sisters, Brothers, Role in the Clan or Tribe.

Then in interest groups or individually, do a quickwrite where they put their character into the setting and develop the plot. If this is being written as observational writing (memoir or autobiographical) review characteristics from the narrative and have students start the rough draft.

When finished, return to original seats and read around with yellow highlighter of positive language or ideas. Read around for revising suggestions, write on seperate Post-It or paper. The teacher makes sure that these are done quickly; do not belabor this. Final editing can be done with read-arounds or three-before-me editing.

Ear-to-Ear-Reading

Ear-to-ear reading was first presented by Jim Rogers in the CIRC model of cooperative learning in reading.

What it is

It is a form of partner reading that lowers the affective filter. As CIRC research shows, sometimes, with some cultures and struggling readers, the eye to eye reading is threatening.

How to do it

Two students place their chairs side by side, but the seats face in opposite directions. When the students are sitting in the chairs,

171

their heads and ears are close together, but their faces are facing the opposite direction. Each partner has the same reading material and they take turns reading to each other from that passage. (Hint: we have found that sentence by sentence forces them to stay focused. If each one reads a whole paragraph, the other tends to phase out.)

Learning logs (often called reading logs)

What they are

With some adaptation the reading log is useful in all content areas. We have the students keep all assigned seat work, homework, and responses to readings in this log. It saves on management. We think of the learning log as content-based and teacher-assigned. As such, it is collected regularly and assessed.

How to use it

The students have a set of $8\frac{1}{2}$" by 11" unlined sheets of paper, about five or six to begin with. The first sheet has a line down the middle with the words *Text* on one side and *You* on the other. After the first page, the student can draw the line down the middle and write *Text* and *You*. Sometimes we don't want them to make the line down the middle. The strategy "Sketch and Listen" is a good example. We want the students sketching the picture in their head, as such; lines anywhere would interfere with that picture. Wanting students to practice clustering and mind-mapping leads to no-lines paper. Use lined paper when you want strictly writing (and they can staple those to the back of their learning log).

Quicksketch

What it is

As its name implies, quicksketch is the drawing form of a quickwrite. It is done as a right brain activity that can demonstrate comprehension without the use of words. Students learn that sketching is different than drawing. We use sketching to use all parts of our brain to produce language. A new twist on sketching: Don't think of writing first and then drawing or drawing first and then writing. Instead, encourage the students to make it a back and forth process—sketch, write, think, rewrite, resketch, rethink. Many noteworthy authors, E. B. White included, used this method when writing.

Variations

This has lead to strategies such as "Listen and Sketch" and "Sketch and Write," described earlier.

Picture dictionary/cognitive dictionary

What it is

Both of these are excellent personal dictionaries for ELD students. The picture dictionary is, perhaps, more appropriate for the earlier grades. It is a very simple structure, easily reproduced (see graphic). Punch holes in the paper and have students keep this in their reading folder.

Picture Dictionary

bee

The cognitive dictionary involves students in metacognition. It is a grid that asks the students to predict the meaning of the chosen word, then discuss it with the teacher (done whole class, in teams, and individually). Following that, they sketch or write something in the primary language that will make them remember the meaning (you can only suggest here, your idea of a sketch may not work for their brain). Finally, they use it in a sentence.

Word	Prediction
Sketch or L1	Use in a sentence

Language development cycle

What it is

Teachers have often underestimated student-generated text for beginning reading. The following is a cycle that a teacher, trained aide, or trained parent could follow. We trained our aides in these steps. This did not mean that our aides taught ELD. They only reinforced what we had taught in whole group and in small, ELD groups. This cycle was a way of using our aides most effectively. This is based on a group of five or six emergent readers.

How to do it

1. Read a book concerning the theme being taught. Develop a topic sentence for the students. This will vary depending on the

format you wish to teach, for example, sequencing, retelling, or cause and effect. Students will give you the sentences to follow the topic sentence. Do revising and editing with the students.

2. Make a second copy on sentence strips, and type up the third copy.

3. Pass out a sentence to each student in the group, they read it, match it, and put it in sequence. Encourage your aide not to jump in with the correct answer each time. Help the students discover some skills to figure it out. At this stage, it is usually matching.

4. Cut sentences into phrases, having the students count the words in each phrase. They remake the paragraph if the paragraph is very long. This is the place to work with about 4-5 sentences from the paragraph.

5. Cut phrases into words, have students put them back in order and read.

6. Make up new sentences with word cards.

7. Students and aide (teacher) identify key vocabulary on original chart and pull those word cards.

8. Adult uses these word cards to teach and practice any decoding, contextual, or semantic skills.

9. These word cards can be used for games and reading activities from cloze technique to spelling.

10. The original frame always remains whole and visible.

Metacognitive reading groups (advanced, SDAIE level)

What it is

For the more advanced reading groups, who still need some processing, but are working from grade level texts, we often follow these steps.

How to do it

1. As you pull the group, ask students to predict what words they will find in the selection they will read. Reference all the language around the walls. Chart the words they predict on a chart that remains visible to them during this process. (Students often have a higher oral vocabulary than reading. This provides a bridge between the two.)

2. Following the SQ3R model, begin by having students look at pictures and titles and predict what they think it will be about. Then they skim the first page (or so), come back and discuss if their predictions were correct. After you have modeled this, use the Modified SQ3R for partners (Project GLAD).

3. Before you send them off to read either silently or in partners, give them small Post-It notes. These are for "clunkers" and "links." Clunkers are words that students are not sure of (meaning or pronunciation) and links are for words from our walls, words they feel are high level, or words that remind them of something they have read. We use these for two reasons: We cannot have students underlining and highlighting textbooks; and even with our higher leveled groups, if you send them off to read, they never remember or acknowledge words they had trouble with. This way, the Post-Its seem to take the onus off those kinds of words. The link words provide you with some possible areas of books to recommend to students for personal reading.

4. Pull the students back in a group and process "clunkers" and "links," and continue with other reading skills as diagnosed.

Interactive journals

"I'm just talking about this because my mom and dad are getting a divorce. And I feel like I'm stuck in the middle and can't get out. Please read and sign.

> How do the stars twinkle so bright
> Why do people run for the light?
> How come people are scared in dark places?
> And how come I feel so bad about my parents separation?"

> — reprinted from a third grade interactive journal

What they are

Interactive journals provide an opportunity for students to engage in silent sustained writing and sketching, either content-based or personal issues (as evidenced by the quote). This strategy offers a chance for students to engage in a written dialogue with the teacher about issues meaningful to them. The teacher's response must show real interest in the message being expressed, not merely to offer bland compliments about handwriting or spelling.

How to use them

Have five sheets of unlined paper stapled together. Allow 15 or so minutes for response. In the younger grades, the teacher always models the journal writing either with teacher journaling or interactive writing. Gabrielle Rico provides a trigger word for a prompt from which students work by clustering first. We have not found that necessary when our walls are dripping with language and content that the students have created.

In the early years, or with non-readers, it is crucial that the teacher write back with the student watching, thus providing one more opportunity for modeled, guided writing. To do this, start a Reading/Writing Choice Time. First the students must write to you in their journal, then they turn their journal upside down on their desks and go off to a reading/writing choice. When you are ready, call the student back to respond with them watching. This avoids those deadly lines of young students waiting for the teacher to respond. Value and encourage the students practice and use of "transitional spelling" (once called inventive spelling); this is phonics in practice.

With older students, you can take the journals home, respond and return them the next day. We usually fade this out once we start Writer's Workshop, due to lack of time. We always keep the option open for students to write to us and leave their journal on our desk.

Appendix 1

Glossary of Terms

Affective filter. A construct developed to refer to the effects of personality, motivation, anxiety, and other variables in second language acquisition. These variables interact with others to raise or lower the affective filter in a classroom. When anxiety, low self-esteem, or low motivation are present in a classroom, the filter is high, thus inhibiting acquisition.

Basic interpersonal communicative skills. A construct originally developed by James Cummins to refer to aspects of language proficiency strongly associated with basic communication and oral fluency. Basic interpersonal communication skills are not highly correlated to literacy and academic achievement. Young students often achieve this early and effortlessly, but this does not ensure school success.

Cognitive/academic language proficiency. A construct, also suggested by James Cummins, that refers to the aspects of language proficiency strongly related to literacy and academic achievement. This theory helps teachers to understand why ELL could "speak without an accent" and still fail in school. This level of language must be taught and practiced by students.

Comprehensible input. Steven Krashen's hypothesis to describe language that is understandable and meaningful, usually when directed at second-language learners. Comprehensible input is characterized as language that the second-language learner already knows plus a range of new language which is made understandable by the use of certain strategies. This is reinforced by Vygotsky's Zone of Proximal Development (scaffolding information, 1962).

ELD. English Language Development (formerly ESL)

ELL. English Language Learner (formerly LEP)

Integrated curriculum. Curriculum that interrelates listening, speaking, reading, and writing, and integrates language across the curriculum.

L1. Primary language or the first language spoken by a student.

Scaffolding. A theory developed from the work of Vygotsky (1962). It proposes that it is crucial to provide ELLs with certain strategies that provide support until they are academically fluent, hence, scaffold as when building a bridge.

Semantic clues. Clues that help a student in reading by using meaning-based strategies.

Syntactic clues. Clues that help a student in reading by using strategies based on knowledge of language patterns, grammatical structures.

Total Physical Response (TPR). An approach from Asher that utilizes the body and movement to indicate comprehension rather than speaking. A key approach for students in the silent period of language acquisition, for whom forced-speaking creates anxiety.

Appendix 2

Sample Daily Lesson Plans

This appendix illustrates a sample day and several sample daily lesson plans to give you an idea of how to implement this approach in the classroom. Remember, these are just guidelines. The amount of time you use it in your classroom will depend on the amount of integration in your program. Obviously, if you are a middle school teacher, yours will look different for 50- or 100-minute blocks. Set aside time for your "must do's" and let the rest of the day assume a natural flow based on where you are in your unit. Not all strategies are at their most effective at any place during the unit.

Today, with *balanced literacy,* teaching seems to stress equal number of minutes every day for each strategy, regardless of students' needs. Our vision is that our second language learners need more focusing/motivation activities (accessing and building background information) and teacher input (direct teaching) at the beginning of a unit. Furthermore, that content-based reading and writing is more effective after this has been built. Thus, we will see more content-based teacher talk at the beginning of a unit and more content-based student talking, reading, and writing toward the end.

Sample Daily Lesson Plan 1
Chickens Aren't the Only Ones
(generally kindergarten through first)

Day 1

Focusing and motivation

- Standards: Portfolios
- Big Book: The Important Thing About Eggs, discuss
- Observation charts: Kinds of egg layers, process orally
- Inquiry charts: What do you know about egg layers? What do you want to know?
- Poetry: "Eggs Here"

Input

- Narrative input: 2 x—act out change ending
- Personal interaction: Which ending do you like?
- Poetry: "I Know an Unusual Egg"
  – Learning log: Sketch favorite ending—what animal?
- Strip book: Eggs Can

Guided oral practice

- T-graph: Respect
- Picture file: Share and discuss, then categorize prediction of born alive and not—model interactive writing with team responses
- Poetry: "Born Alive"

Reading/writing

- Model journaling and the process of "write to me," then go to a reading/writing choice that includes: narrative, research corner, literacy events, science notes, to name a few.

Closure

- Reread charts/poetry
- Home-school connection
- Work jobs

Day 2

Focusing and motivation

- Poetry: Read and highlight
- Review narrative with word cards
- Read aloud: "Chickens Aren't the Only Ones"—10/2

Input

- Pictorial: 10/2 —process of hatching learning log
- Graphic organizer: Total class—predict categories
- Poetry: "Is This Oviparous?"

Guided oral practice

- Farmer in the dell
- Chant this many times (one to two weeks, depending on class)
- Reading from words cards
- Flip chant

Reading/writing

- Flexible group reading : **Model** team tasks—(team banner and name, team picture of as many oviparous animals as possible, team mind-map with sketch, team pocket poetry)
  - *Eggs Here, Eggs There* book—skills, as appropriate e.g., letters/sounds
- Poetry: Chant again

- Reading /writing workshop: journals first; add work with farmer and dell, team and own flip chants, *Eggs Here* book, author's chair

Closure

- Home-school connection: Tell parents about two oviparous animals and sketch them.
- Poetry: Teams chant
- Add to inquiry or observation charts: Make changes of predictions or grammar.

Day 3

Focusing and motivation

- Highlight poetry
- Add word cards to pictorial and animals to graphic organizers
- Chant "Farmer in the Dell"
- Process home-school connection

Input

- Shared reading: Hatched from an Egg
- Expert groups: Heterogeneous—oviparous animals
- Team tasks: Add team words and pictures to add to Living Wall
- Team graphic organizer with sketch and write

Guided oral practice

- Process Grid - heads together
- Poetry: Is this oviparous?
- Group frame: There are many oviparous animals
  - Use this time for modeled writing. Verbalize what you are doing.
  - Respond, revise, and edit as appropriate.

Reading/writing

- Flexible group reading
  - Team tasks (add two new animals and habitat, poetry booklet at listening center, team farmer in dell, team process grid)
  - Guided reading: Hatched from an Egg
- Poetry: "I'm a Frog, Small and Brown"
- Reading/writing workshop: Start with journals
  - Mini-lesson
  - Author's chair

Closure

- Review
- Zoo discussion: Invite them to bring pictures of or stuffed zoo animals.
- Home-school connection: Parents' favorite zoo animals

Day 4

Focusing and motivation

- Reread paragraph, highlight and make changes.
- "Hello My Name Is Joe and I work in an Egg Factory" chant
- Process home-school connections.

Input

- Discussion about why we have zoos
- Living Wall: Zoo, build together.
- If I Ran the Zoo: 10/2
  - Learning log: Create an imaginary animal.

Reading/writing

- Flexible reading
  - Team tasks: Team zoo and team animals to add to Living Wall
  - Skills: Guided reading from strip paragraph; skills as diagnosed
- Reading/writing workshop: Start with journals.
  - Add checkbooks and phone pad for veterinarian, subscriptions.
- Interactive writing: Big Book of oviparous animals
- Chalkboard phonics with mistakes from the interactive writing

Closure

- Review poetry.
- Share team tasks, process behaviors on T-graph.
- Home-school connection : With parents, create an imaginary zoo animal.

Day 5

Focusing and motivation

- Review poetry and add word cards and conversation bubbles to narrative.
- Read the walls (focused reading); write walls with chalk board.
- "I Can Spell Ant …..ant" chant (use phonemes and morphemes as appropriate)

Reading and writing

- Chalkboard phonics: Total group or flexible reading
- Modeled writing: "If I Ran the Zoo"—using a frame
- Letter to Zoo: Ask questions and ask how we can help
- Personal interaction: Own ideas
- Big Book: The important thing—by teams, dictate to teachers and draw pictures to match
- Reading /writing workshop start with journals

Closure

- Review and highlight charts, especially Inquiry and observation charts.
- Letter home
- Evaluate week
- "We just know what we've been told"

Reptiles
Animal Classification: Same and Different
Sample Daily Lesson Plan

Day 1 (overview and snakes)

Focus and motivation

- Big Book: Shared reading
- Super Scientist Awards: Standards
- Inquiry charts: What do we know about reptiles? What else do you want to know? How can we find out?
- Poetry: Reptiles here
- Observation chart: Various kinds of reptiles
- Portfolios: Colored dots (heterogeneous groups), numbered off

Input

- Tree of life: Mind-map, focus of reptiles and their characteristics
- Narrative input chart: A day in the life of
- Observation of real snake
- Snake poem
- Read aloud: Zoo books

Guided oral practice

- T-graph: Cooperation
- Picture file activities: Reptile or not, numbered heads together—one sentence
- Invite teams to come up with team names/Discuss issue team wants most to learn about.
- Personal interaction: Do you like reptiles? Which one do you like best? Least?

Reading/writing/language arts

- Writer's Workshop
  - Mini-lesson: Authentic literacy events, strip book
  - Author's chair
- Flexible group reading
  - Guided reading or running record
  - Team tasks
    * Team banner
    * Team name
    * Team picture
    * Team mind map

Closure

- Interactive journals/*Teacher Models*
- Read aloud: Reptiles Are
- Reread inquiry charts, poetry, and input charts.
- Work jobs
- Home-school connection: In your neighborhood, take a survey of reptiles.

Day 2 (turtles)

Focus and motivation

- Review with word cards.
- Learning logs
- Read aloud
- Highlight high-level words in the poetry.
- Inquiry chart: Add and make changes.
- Act out review of narrative.

Input

- Comparative input chart: Turtle and tortoise
  - Learning log
  - ELD review
- Poetry
  - Is this oviparous? Yes, Ma'am (use pictures of animals).

Guided oral practice

- Teams brainstorm animals.
  - Total class graphic organizer: 10/2 with primary language
  - They predict categories.
- Farmer in the Dell
  - Reptiles
  - Word cards—take to making "interesting" sentences and read
  - Flip chant

Reading/writing/language arts

- Journals
- Reading/writing workshop
  - Add unit theme books, pocket poetry, retelling of narrative, etc.
  - Author's chair

- Flexible grouping
  - Guided reading of poetry booklet
  - Team tasks
    * Team flip chant
    * Team farmer in the dell
    * Team sentences from farmer in the dell
    * Team listening center (poetry booklet on tape)

Closure

- Share team tasks and review group behaviors based on T-graph.
- Review charts.
- Home-school connection: Retell the narrative input to your parents—what ending do they like?

Day 3 (lizards and crocodilians)

Focus and motivation

- Highlight poetry.
- Add to graphic organizer: Word cards; L1 review
- Farmer in the Dell: Chant and add more words.

Input

- Expert groups: Heterogeneous reading groups—types of lizards, crocs
- Team tasks: Team graphic organizer, team story map of narrative
- Process grid
- Group Frame or Cooperative strip paragraph—expository, compare and contrast
- Read aloud—Zoo books
- Process home-school connection.

Reading/writing/language arts

- Journals
- Reading/writing workshop: Mini-lesson on editing checklist
- Flexible group reading: Cooperative strip paragraph—top two groups; metacognitive reading groups
- Team tasks: Add process grid.
- Sketch and listen in learning log. You cover pictures, and students sketch as you read. Stop every two or three paragraphs.

Closure

- Review charts.
- Invite kids to bring reptiles for the herpetarium next day.
- Home-school connection: Interview parents on favorite reptile.

Day 4

Focus and motivation

- Ear-to-ear reading with poetry booklet
- Add to process grid.
- Golden Pen award
- Process charts and home-school connections.

Input

- Comparative: lizard and crocodile
- Fictional story about lizards or crocodiles
- Total class story map

Guided oral practice

- Picture file
  - Categorize reptile species, add to process grid.

- Strip book
- Brainstorm storytelling ideas in teams.

Reading/writing/language arts

- If I Ran the Zoo: Read aloud.
  - Learning log : Create a Seuss-like reptile.
- Reading/writing workshop
- Journals
- Literacy materials for a herpetarium
- Flexible group reading
  - Emergent readers with cooperative strip paragraph (skill teaching)
- Team task: Add animals to add to zoo, labels
  - Team story map

Closure

- Poetry
- Review zoo information
- Home-school connection: Ask parents or friends about fictional stories they remember about reptiles.

Day 5 (dinosaurs and tuataras)

Focus and motivation

- Process inquiry charts and home-school connections.
- Poems
- Process grid/zoo
- Focused reading
- Read aloud: Lunch at the Zoo.
- "Hello, my name is Joe, and I work in a Herpetarium" chant

Input

- Letter to zoo: Total class
  - How can we help?
  - Action plan
- Big Book tasks: either "Reptiles are using metaphors" or "The Important Book"
- Model—total class
- Students, write
  - Respond
  - Edit
  - Art

Reading/writing/language arts

- Framed inquiry letter home
- Reading/writing workshop
- Cross-age reading
- Flexible group reading: leveled groups
- Team tasks: Previously required tasks
- Prepare students for individual tasks.

Closure

- Review.
- Evaluate week.
- Make end of the week changes to the inquiry charts.

#2
SPACE
SAMPLE DAILY LESSON PLAN
(generally grades three through four)

Day 1

Focus and motivation

- Astronomer awards with key vocabulary
- Poetry: "Stars Here"
- Space buttons
- Inquiry charts: What do you know about space? What would you like to learn?
- Line-up planets: Order, size representation, distance apart (put on charts). Review.
- Observation charts on each planet
- Poetry: "I Know an Unusual Planet"
- Portfolios with dots

Input

- The Nature of the Solar System, using picture book and pictorial input chart, black paper, colored chalk, word cards, orbits
- 10/2 lecture with primary language
- Read aloud: Issac Asimov's series on the universe

Guided oral practice

- T-graph: Respect, team points
- Picture file cards: Observe, discuss—most interesting modeled writing
- Personal interaction: Would you like to explore space? Why? Why not?

Input

- Pictorial input: Birth of a star—10/2 with primary language
- Poetry: "Stars Here, Stars There"

Reading and writing

- Learning log activity: Teacher models
- Flexible group reading
  - Guided reading or running record
  - Team tasks: Sketch and label birth and kinds of stars.
    * Team name and banner
    * Team mind map

Writer's workshop

- Mini-lesson: Class gathering—kinds of writing
- Write
- Author's chair

Closure

- Interactive journal writing
- Reread charts.
- Home-school connection: With parents/siblings observe/draw stars you see
- Work jobs

Day 2

Focus and motivation

- Review with word cards.
- Highlight poetry and processs home-school connection.
- Important Book of the Sun

- Read aloud: Asimov's Birth and Death of a Sun
- Ongoing prediction and movement of the Birth and Death of Sun to music

Input

- Graphic organizer on Sun as a Star and the center of the galaxy and other galaxies: 10/2 primary language
- *Sun*, Seymore Simon
- Learning log response and ELD or primary language review

Input

- Narrative input chart: Sentron (science fiction genre)
  - Story map
  - Guided team story map (retelling)

Guided oral practice

- Farmer in the Dell—Stars
  - Reading
  - Flip chant

Reading/writing

- Team Writing Workshop
  1. Using story-map strips, teams brainstorm story on strips.
  2. Teacher models highlighting good qualities: Teams do read-arounds—highlight and share.
  3. Teacher models revising: Teams do revising suggestions with one or two other teams (orally or on Post-It notes)—share.
  4. Teacher models editing and revising suggestions: Teams make editing suggestions with one other team (orally or on Post-It notes)—share.

5. Each team makes final revising and editing decisions: One person recopies and other(s) illustrate.
6. Publishers' share.
- Flexible group reading
  - Guided reading of poetry book
  - Team tasks
    * Team flip chant
    * Team farmer in the dell
    * Team listening center (poetry booklet on tape)
- Writer's workshop
  - Mini-lesson: Class gathering on how to use story map strips
  - Write
  - Author's chair

Closure

- Personal Interaction: Choose a kind of star and say if you think it could support life somewhere in space. Why? Why not?
- Journal writing
- Home-school connection: Interview parents about stars—what do they know? Do they remember any stories or sayings about stars?

Day 3

Focus and motivation

- Class strip book: Stars can, but stars cannot . . .
- Process home-school connections.
- Interest pieces: Put up parents stories and sayings.
- Poetry: "Stars Are Reindeer" poems
- Inquiry charts: Process.

Input

- Expert groups (heterogeneous reading/processing/study skills)
  - Different galaxies or comets, asteroids, meteors, galaxies
- Team tasks
  - Team picture of Milky Way, team mind map of stars, team strip book, and Important Book Frame

Guided oral practice

- Stand and chant.
- Process grid: Numbered heads together to answer

Reading/writing

- Cooperative strip paragraph: Comparing and contrasting
  - Respond, revise, and edit.
- Ear-to-ear reading from poetry booklet
- Writer's workshop
  - Mini-lesson: class gathering, editing checklist
  - Write
  - Author's chair

Closure

- Process Inquiry charts
- Home-school connection: Interest pieces from magazines, newspapers, and so on

Day 4

Focusing and motivation

- Read aloud : Orion stories from several cultures
- Focused reading: Read and write the walls.

Reading/writing

- Flexible group reading with cooperative strip paragraph: Two groups—advanced group
  - Metacognitive reading groups
  - Team tasks: Process grid, team cooperative paragraph, and Big Book chalk illustrations.
- Poetry
- Listen and sketch: Discuss "pictures in your mind."
- Reading and writing workshop
  - Mini-lesson: Class gathering on reading/writing workshop
  - Write/read
  - Author's chair

Closure

- Personal Interaction: What do you think about space aliens? Why?
- Journal writing
- Home-school connection: Interview family/friends—What was their favorite science fiction movie/book? Why? Do they think that there is life in space?

Day 5

Input

- Read aloud: Native American legend explaining stars (Keepers of the Earth)
- Read/write the walls: Cognitive or picture dictionary
- Process charts and home-school connections.

Reading/writing

- Flexible group reading: One group—emergent readers from cooperative strip paragraph; the other, an ELD group creates their own group frame.

- Teams finish team tasks.
- Share.
- Team Big Books: Team illustrations, two or three "team" items
- Reading/writing workshop
  - Mini-lesson: class gathering on publishing
  - Write/read
  - Author's chair

Guided oral practice

- Team oral practice for oral presentation

Closure

- Process all charts.
- Framed inquiry letter home to parents
- Group/personal interpretation of poem or story
- Share Big Books.
- Space Ice Cream
- Evaluate week.
- Teacher and student-generated quizzes
- Learning logs assessed

Appendix 3

Tried Topics and Resources

Tried topics (Remember, these are only a few possibilities.)

Some are themes; some are content areas.

Literature

The Wolf Through Fact and Fiction; or Fish: Legends
  Around the World
Comparative fairy tales
Comparative biographies: The American West
Poetry around the curricula: Found poetry, shell poetry,
  haiku, and so on
Survival
Explorations
Explaining and teaching
Communities around the world
Books like *Island of the Blue Dolphin, Chickens Aren't the
  Only Ones, Molly's Pilgrim, Oranges*, and so on

Social studies

My world (from myself to school to community to world)
Comparative Native Americans
Changes: Events in history

Our roots: Cultural heritage
Forces in history: Immigration, war, and people
Prehistoric people
The Middle Ages
World hunger
The birth of Islam
Earliest Americans

Science

The world around me: Matter, energy, and me
Interdependence and independence of living things
Ocean life: Many subtopics, too numerous to name
Oceanography: Affecting our life
Life in the Pond
Ecosystems: From desert to ocean
Birds of prey
Endangered planet: To include endangered animals, trees, and humans
Space
Solar systems
Exploring inside: Ourselves, atoms, and the earth

Resources

In poetry

Shel Silverstein
Jack Prelutsky
Myra Cohen Livingston
Natalia Belting

In language

Brian Cutting: *Language is Fun*
McCrackens: *Theme books, Reading is Just the Tiger's Tail*

Leanna Traill: *Highlighting Their Strengths* or anything
Andrea Butler: anything
Lucy Calkins: *The Art of Teaching Writing* or anything

Theory

Joan Wink, Critical Pedagogy; *Notes from the Real World*
Frank Smith: Anything
Donald Graves: Anything
Jeanne Chall: Anything
Kenneth Goodman: Anything
Dorothy Strickland: Especially articles from *Reading Teacher*
The Reading Teacher: Best all-around newest strategies and
    information
Transitions or Invitations: Reggie Routeman
Jim Trelease: Read aloud
Gabrielle Rico: *Writing the Natural Way*
M. Adams: *Beginning to Read*
J. Shefelbine: *A Reading Framework*
New Reading Task Force and ELA Framework
ELA and ELD Standards
Science and History/Social Science Frameworks

Teacher resources

San Diego *Zoobooks*
National Geographic magazines, films, videos, and so on
Ranger Rick magazines, especially "Nature Scope" for
    teachers
National Geographic World
World Wildlife Foundation
Arbor Day Foundations
Consulates from different countries
Chamber of Commerce from different cities
Representatives from different textbook companies
Laser discs: *World Civilization* and *Windows on Science*

Internet: Especially the *LA Times* web sites
Grollier's and Encarta CD Encyclopedias

Practical resources for teachers

Eyewitness books

Animals, Jim Harter, Dover Press

Scholastic Rhyming Dictionary

Zoobooks

"Naturescope," by *Ranger Rick*

Poetry: Shel Siverstein, Jack Prelutsky

References

Adams, Marilyn, *Beginning to Read, Thinking and Learning About Print*, MIT Press, 1995.

Berman, et al., "Meeting the Challenge of Language Diversity," California Legislature, 1991.

Blanton, William E. and Mormon, Gary B., "Research Relevant to Learning from Information Texts." A paper presented at the IRA Conference, Anaheim CA, September 1987.

Brechtel, Marcia, *Bringing the Whole Together*, Dominie Press, San Diego, CA, 1992.

Butler and Turnbill, *Towards a Reading-Writing Classroom*, Heinemann, 1984.

California State Department of Education, *Crossing the Schoolhouse Border*.

California State Department of Education, "English Language Arts Framework," 1998.

California State Department of Education, "Every Child a Reader: the California Reading Task Force" and "Reading Advisory," Sacramento, CA, 1995 and 1996.

Calkins, L., *The Art of Teaching Writing*, Heinemann, 1986.

Chall, Jeanne S., *Learning to Read: The Great Debate*, New York, McGraw Hill, 1983.

Chall, Jeanne S., *Stages of Reading Development*, New York, McGraw Hill, 1983.

Chamot and O'Malley, *The CALLA Handbook*, Addison-Wesley, 1994.

Clay, Marie, *Becoming Literate*, Heinemann, 1991, and *An Observation Survey of Early Literacy Achievement*, 1993.

Clymer, T., *The Utility of Phonic Generalizations in the Primary Grades*, Reading Teacher, Vol. 50, 1996.

Cody, Betty and Nelson, David, *Teaching Elementary Language Arts*, Belmont, CA, Wadsworth, 1982.

Collier and Thomas: 1995, *Longitudinal Study of Successful Programs for Second Language Learners.*

Commission on Reading, *Becoming a Nation of Readers*, Washington, D.C., National Institute of Education, 1984.

Costa, Art, "What Human Beings Do When They Behave Intelligently and How Can They Become More So," California State University, Sacramento, 1981.

Cummins, J., *Empowering Minority Students*, CABE, 1989, and *Negotiating Identities* (Cummins and Swain), CABE, 1996.

Cummins, J., "Knowledge, Power and Identity in Teaching English as a Second Language," Draft, CABE, 1991.

Elkind, D., *The Hurried Child*, Boston, Addison-Wesley, 1981.

"Every Child's Right: Literacy," *Reading Teacher*, October, 1991.

Farr and Tone, "Portfolio and performance assessment," Harcourt Brace, 1994.

Flood, Lapp, et al., *Handbook of Research on Teaching English Language Arts*, IRA, 1991.

Frager, A. M., "How Good Are Content Area Teachers' Judgments of Reading Abilities of Secondary School Students?" *Journal of Reading*, Vol. 27, #5, February 1984.

Good, Thomas L. and Brophy, Jere E., "Analyzing Classroom Interaction: A More Powerful Alternative," *Educational Technology*, November, 1971.

Goodman, Kenneth, Ed., *The Psycholinguistic Nature of the Reading Process*, Detroit, Wayne State University Press, 1973. Miscue Analysis

Goodman, Kenneth, Ed., *What's Whole in Whole Language*, Heinemann, 1986.

Graves, Donald, *Writing: Teachers and Children at Work*, Heinemann, 1982.

Hansen, J. and Hubbard, R., "Poor Readers Can Draw Inferences," *The Reading Teacher*, #7, March 1984.

Heathington, B. S. and Alexander, J. E., "Do Classroom Teachers Emphasize Attitudes Towards Reading?" *Reading Teacher*, #6, February 1984.

Honig, Bill, *The New California Schools*, Sacramento, July 5, 1983.

Joyce, Showers, and Rolheiser-Bennett, "Staff Development and Student Learning: A Synthesis of Research on Models of Teaching, Educational Leadership," October 1987.

Kovalik, Susan, Remarks, Mentor Teacher Conference, Anaheim, CA, 1986.

Krashen, S., *Second Language Learning and Second Language Acquisition*, Alemany Press, 1981.

Krashen, S., *The Natural Approach*, Alemany Press, 1983.

Library of Congress, *Books in Our Future*, 1984.

Macro Press, *Exploring Science*, 1992.

McCrackens, B. and M., *Reading Is Just the Tiger's Tail.*

McTighe and Wiggins, G., *Understanding by Design*, ASCD, 1998.

Ramirez, D., "Final Report: Longitudinal Study of Structured English Immersion, Early-exit and Late-exit Bilingual Programs," U.S. Department of Education, 1991.

Rico, Gabriele, *Writing the Natural Way*, Tarcher, Inc., 1983.

Schooling and the Language Minority Student: A Theoretical Framework, California State Department of Education, CSULA, 1981.

Shefelbine, J., *Learning and Using Phonics in Beginning Reading,* New York, Scholastic, Inc., 1995

Smith, Frank, *Reading Without Nonsense*, Teachers College Press, Columbia University, 1985.

Smith, Frank, *Insult to Intelligence*, Arbor House, 1986.

Stahl, Steven, "Saying the 'P' Word: Nine Guidelines for Exemplary Phonic Instruction," *The Reading Teacher,* April 1992.

Trail, Leanna, *Highlight My Strengths,* Rigby, 1995.

Willert, Mary K. and Kamil, Constance, "Reading in Kindergarten," Young Children, May 1985.

Wink, Joan, *Critical Pedagogy; Notes from the Real World*, New York, Longman, 1997.

Winograd, Peter and Greenlee, Marilyn, "Students Need a Balanced Reading Program," Educational Leadership, Vol. 43, #7, April 1986.

Wong, Fillmore L., "Pacific Perspectives on Language Learning and Teacher," TESOL, Washington, D.C., 1982.

Yopp, H. "Developing Phonemic Awareness in Young Children," *Reading Teacher*, Vol. 45 (1992).

Vygotsky, L.S., *Thought and Language,* MIT Press, 1962.

Zirkelback, T., "A Personal View of Early Reading," *The Reading Teacher*, #6, February 1984.

Practical resources for teachers

Eyewitness books

Animals, Jim Harter, Dover Press

Scholastic Rhyming Dictionary

Zoobooks

"Naturescope," by *Ranger Rick*

Poetry: Shel Siverstein, Jack Prelutsky